PIANTA
DI
ROMA

ROME

MEMORIES OF TIMES PAST

7o PAINTINGS BY ALBERTO PISA

WRITTEN BY RICHARD BOSWORTH
WITH COLIN INMAN AND JOIE DAVIDOW

Thunder Bay Press
An imprint of the Advantage Publishers Group
10350 Barnes Canyon Road, San Diego, CA 92121
www.thunderbaybooks.com

Library of Congress Cataloging-in-Publication Data

Bosworth, R. J. B.
Memories of times past : Rome / written by Richard Bosworth, with Colin Inman and Joie Davidow.
p. cm.
Includes bibliographical references.
ISBN-13: 978-1-59223-865-1
ISBN-10: 1-59223-865-3
1. Rome (Italy)--Description and travel. 2. Rome (Italy)--In art.
3. Pisa, Alberto. I. Inman, Colin. II. Davidow, Joie. III. Title.
DG806.I56 2008
945'.632091--dc22
2008017969

Project manager   John Button
Design manager   Lucy Guenot

Set in Centaur and Gill Sans by Bookcraft Ltd., Stroud, Gloucestershire, United Kingdom

1 2 3 4 5 12 11 10 09 08

Printed in China by Imago

A NOTE TO THE READER

In order to keep the pages of the book as uncluttered as possible,
all sources, notes, and captions relating to illustrations other than
the main paintings have been grouped at the end of the book, and
will be found on pages 173–174.

The front endpaper is taken from *Nuovissima Pianta di Roma, con tutte
le linee delle Tramvie, degli Omnibus, Tramvia dei Castetti Romani e di Civita
Castellana* of 1909. The back endpaper is taken from Plate 13 of
Keith Johnstone's *Royal Atlas of Modern Geography*, published in 1905.

CONTENTS

5 Rome 1905   Richard Bosworth

19 Alberto Pisa, 1864–1936   Colin Inman

22 Temple of Saturn from the Basilica Julia in the Forum

24 The Forum from the Arch of Septimius Severus

26 The Forum, Looking Towards the Capitol

28 Marble Relief of the Ambarvalia Sacrifice, in the Forum

30 St. Peter's and Castel Sant'Angelo from the Tiber

32 Temple of Saturn from the Portico of the Dii Consentes

34 A Corner of the Forum from the Base of the Temple of Saturn

36 Temple of Mars Ultor

38 Temple of Vespasian from the Portico of the Dii Consentes

40 The Colosseum on a Spring Day

42 The Colosseum at Sunset

44 Arch of Titus

46 A Procession in the Catacomb of Callistus

48 Flavian Basilica on the Palatine

50 Library of the House of Domitian on the Palatine

52 Forum of Nerva

54 Fountain of Trevi

56 Column of Marcus Aurelius, Piazza Colonna

58 Pantheon, a Flank View

60 Silversmiths' Arch in the Velabrum

62 Convent Garden of San Cosimato, Vicovaro

64 A Tract of the Claudian Aqueduct Outside the City

66 Campagna Romana, from Tivoli

68 Subiaco from the Monastery of St. Benedict

70 Garden of the Monastery of Santa Scholastica, Subiaco

72 Holy Stairs at the Sacro Speco

74 Little Gleaner in the Campagna

76 Sea Horse Fountain in the Villa Borghese

78 Ornamental Water, Villa Borghese

80 Village Street at Anticoli, in the Sabine Hills

82 Villa d'Este, Tivoli

84 In Villa Borghese

86 The Spanish Steps, Piazza di Spagna

88 At the Foot of the Spanish Steps, Piazza di Spagna, on a Wet Day

90 Roman Peasant Carrying Copper Water Pot

92 Chapel of the Passion in the Church of San Clemente

94 A Rustic Dwelling in the Roman Campagna

96 Procession with the Host at Subiaco

98 Girl Selling Birds in the Via del Campidoglio

100 Entrance to Ara Coeli from the Forum

102 In the Church of Ara Coeli

104 Doorway of the Monastery of St. Benedict (Sagro Speco) at Subiaco

106 Chapel of San Lorenzo Loricato at St. Benedict's, Subiaco

108 Steps of the Dominican Nuns' Church of Saints Domenico and Sisto

110 Porta San Paolo

112 The Colosseum in a Storm

114 Arch of Titus from the Arch of Constantine

116 Medieval House at Tivoli

118 Ilex Avenue and Fountain (Fontana Scura), Villa Borghese

120 "House of Cola di Rienzo," by Ponte Rotto

122 San Clemente, Choir and Tribune of Upper Church

124 Santa Maria in Cosmedin

126 Chapel of San Zeno (Orto del Paradiso) in San Prassede

128 Cloisters of St. Paul's-Without-the-Walls

130 Cloisters in Santa Scholastica, Subiaco

132 Santa Maria Sopra Minerva

134 St. Peter's

136 Interior of St. Peter's, the Bronze Statue of St. Peter

138 A Cardinal in Villa d'Este

140 Villa d'Este—Path of the Hundred Fountains

142 Theatre of Marcellus

144 Island of the Tiber—the Isola Sacra

146 The Steps of Ara Coeli

148 Steps of the Church of Saints Domenico and Sisto

150 Santa Maria Maggiore

152 Arch of Constantine

154 Castel and Ponte Sant'Angelo

156 Bronze Statue of Marcus Aurelius on the Capitol

158 St. Peter's from the Pincian Gardens

160 From the Terrace of the House of Domitian

162 About the Original Book

164 A New World of Color Printing

173 Sources, Notes, and Captions

175 Bibliography

176 The Times Past Archive, Times Past Web site and Acknowledgments

ROME 1905

RICHARD BOSWORTH

On September 22, 1905, architect Giuseppe Sacconi died of a cerebral hemorrhage. Thirty-five years earlier, almost to the day, the Italian army had poured through the Porta Pia and seized Rome for the nation. His might seem an inconsequential passing. Yet since 1882, Sacconi had been in charge of erecting the city's Victor Emmanuel Monument, symbol of that Liberal era that ran from the Risorgimento, or reunification of Italy, to Benito Mussolini's Fascist dictatorship. The most imposing of Rome's twentieth-century monuments in every respect, it had been planned since King Victor Emmanuel's death in 1878, and begun in 1885. It was opened while still unfinished in June 1911 for the nation's fiftieth anniversary celebrations, and eventually completed by the Fascists. The building's blinding whiteness, its columns and crenellations, its massive statue of the king, its altar to the *patria*, its position athwart the Capitoline Hill, were and remain matters of heated debate and controversy. Officialdom applauded—in 1910 the building was hailed as the *nuovo capitolium fulgens*, or "glowing new capitol." Critics were less impressed; the most sardonic and enduring

The Victor Emmanuel Monument from the Piazza Venezia in an 1899 photochrome (below left), and from *Roma: 32 Acquarelli*, a 1910 picture book (below right).

The Rome of 1905 was scarcely a metropolis to compare with London, Paris, or New York, and until 1911 it remained smaller than Naples and Milan, its Italian rivals. With only 130,000 inhabitants at the end of the Napoleonic era in 1815, Rome had begun to grow in the 1850s, expanding to 226,000 by 1870. Thereafter the population grew more rapidly, doubling by 1905 and surpassing half a million by 1911.

ROMA - LA PIENA DEL 1900 - TEMPIO DI VESTA

The Victor Emmanuel Monument from *Ricordi di Roma: Parte II* (top), and *Roma: 70 Vedute* (bottom); a postcard showing the Tempio di Vesta during the floods of 1900 (far right).

dismissal of the monument came from the nationalist writer Giovanni Papini, who in 1913 branded it a "high-class urinal."

The Victor Emmanuel Monument, and the rival meanings attributed to it, offer a microcosm of Rome's conflicting identities in the decade before Italy's entry into World War I in May 1915. Was the Rome of 1905 a free and liberal city, or was it still yoked to the old centers of power?

The vast majority of the city's people still lived within the city walls. Most were crammed into the Campus Martius, the low-lying part of the city near the Tiber. The celebrated river was still given to regular flooding—in 1878 floodwaters rose so high that a sailing match was held on the Corso. Eventually the Tiber was curbed by ugly modern embankments, but the work took a long time to complete, and in 1900 the new century brought another major inundation.

Before Italian occupation, much of the classical city was still occupied by aristocratic villas, religious institutions, farms, and wasteland. Beggars found precarious sanctuary in the celebrated ruins and in the porches of the hundreds of churches. Flocks of goats were driven in when the city gates were unlocked each morning, while pigs and cows still constituted an everyday part of urban life. The Roman Forum was still called the *campo vaccino*, or "cow pasture," even though serious archaeological work was already under way. Liberal rule brought something approaching regular trash collection, but only in the wealthier and more tourist-frequented parts of the city.

King, Church, and State

The new Liberal state was constitutionally grounded in monarchy. The Quirinal Palace, until 1870 the most favored residence of the popes, now became the abode of kings—Victor Emmanuel II, Umberto I until his assassination in 1900, and Victor Emmanuel III. In 1905 Victor Emmanuel III and his tall Montenegrin wife, Elena, presided over a court regularly expanded by royal children, but with little international shine. Tiny in stature and parsimonious with words, deeds, and charity, the king was fond of hunting, photography, and numismatics.

Catholicism had been recognized as the religion of state ever since Emperor Constantine had won the Battle of the Milvian Bridge on the northern edge of the city in 312 (on October 28, the same day that Mussolini would later march on Rome in 1922). In the fifth century, when barbarian invasions overthrew the vestiges of the Roman empire in the West, the popes emerged to run what survived of the city. Papal power, though shaken by revolutions and Napoleonic occupation, only ended with the Italian invasion in 1870. Even then, successive popes—Pius IX, Leo XIII, and Pius X—still hoped that their temporal power might somehow be restored. In 1900 Leo XIII bewailed the fate of a "holy city under enemy domination," and did nothing to discourage his priests from hailing him as *Papa Re*—"Pope King."

Until their accommodation with Mussolini in 1929, the popes may have continued to call themselves prisoners in the Vatican, but their ceremony was always grander than that of the royal family. Despite the trappings of court, the royals remained an uneasy part of the Roman scene.

Though monarch and church both claimed their respective powers, parliament was the most visible center of political authority in Italy's capital.

King Victor Emmanuel III (left) and with his wife Elena (above); a 1910 postcard celebrating the centenary of the birth of Leo XIII (below left); a 1903 postcard marking the empty papal seat (below right).

The lower house, or Chamber of Deputies, was based in the Palace of Montecitorio; the upper house, or Senate, met at the Palazzo Madama, closer to the river. The country's leading politician was Giovanni Giolitti, an occasional bureaucrat who wondered pessimistically to his daughter whether his task in government was to be a "hunchback's tailor." His critics called him "a parliamentary dictator" and "the minister of crime," complaining that, despite his tactical and manipulative skills, his tolerance of corruption gave Liberalism a bad name. In January 1905 Giolitti was prime minister, but in March he handed the position to the undistinguished Alessandro Fortis. This shuffling of office became a feature of Giolitti's decade-long administration, designed to alleviate short-term pressure on the Prime Minister. Giolitti duly returned to office in May 1906.

He rejoiced in the opinion that rhetoric never did anyone any good, believing that the purpose of Liberalism was to provide sound administration and economic growth. While Giolitti was at the helm, national wealth grew at more than 2 percent annually, a rate that would not be achieved again until the economic miracle of the 1950s.

The hope of Liberalism was expressed in another of the great new buildings of the city, the Ministry of Finance. This massive structure, completed in 1877, faces out onto the Via Venti Settembre, beyond the Quirinal Hill. It quickly earned the ire of English resident Augustus Hare. In his *Walks in Rome*, which ran to twenty-two editions, he wrote, "Since the change of government in 1870 have arisen many of the ugliest buildings of the new town—wide, shadeless streets of featureless, ill-built, stuccoed houses, bearing foolish names connected with Piedmontese history and a wretched square called the Piazza dell'Indipendenza in the construction of which much of interest and of beauty was swept away, though its ill-built houses tumbled down before they were finished. Whilst some of the improvements of the old town are well executed, there is not a single point in the entirely modern Rome which calls for anything but contempt."

BOOM AND BUST

Throughout the 1870s and 1880s, Italians witnessed a construction boom in their capital that seemed full of the hope of modernity. The Via Nazionale had been pushed through to the classical ruins near the Piazza Venezia and the Victor Emmanuel Monument. The Piazza Esedra opened in 1888; its flamboyant statuary of naked naiads was added in 1901. The Central Post Office in Piazza San Silvestro began service in 1878. An iron bridge now spanned the Tiber at Ripetta, and eucalyptus trees, thought to discourage mosquitoes, were planted on Monte Mario. In 1885 archaeologist and town planner Rodolfo Lanciani congratulated his country on having paved eighty-two miles of Roman streets and built 3,094 new houses. While turning over 270,000 cubic feet of soil, they had located 192 ancient marble statues, 266 busts, over 36,000 coins, and more than a thousand inscriptions.

Unfortunately, the boom of the 1880s was followed by the bust of the 1890s, when the national banking system trembled after the collapse of the Banca Romana. The new century brought recovery, but it did not particularly benefit Rome. Modern industrialization took off in the Milan–Turin–Genoa triangle, while capitalist agriculture flourished in the Po valley. Rome lagged well behind. Malaria still afflicted peasants in the Campagna, the marshes beyond the city walls, and many of the poor lived wretchedly in huts or in holes scrabbled in once-classical masonry to the south and east of the Via Appia. Branded as "Ethiopians," their life expectancy was low.

A 1909 map showing the Ministry of Finance and the Piazza dell'Indipendenza (opposite page, top); the Ministry of Finance, built 1872–1877, shown in 1906 (bottom); Giovanni Giolitti, prime minister in 1905 (left); the Via Nationale in 1905 (below); Piazza Esedra with the Fountain of Naiads, a 1900 photograph (bottom).

Scholars with Voluminous Shovel-hats, an engraving by H. Regnault from Francis Wey's *Rome* (above); a 1900 postcard of the Piazza del Populo (right); a 1902 postcard from the Society Against Begging, advertising a festival at the Theatro Argentina (below).

Roma - Piazza del Popolo - Costumi Romani

Rome's dismal surroundings often sparked moralizing. The nationalist writer Alfredo Oriani looked out of his train window as he approached his national capital for the first time. "A melancholy beyond words invaded my soul," he wrote. "I was entering the tomb of a civilization that had drawn me from adolescence. I was penetrating a solitude where silence was more eloquent than any voice, and where the squalor was more majestic than anything that progressed."

RICHER AND POORER

Though a quarter of the adult population was reckoned to be illiterate, within the city walls conditions were better than in most of the surrounding countryside. The Roman garrison numbered more than 12,000 soldiers; a fifth of Rome's inhabitants were workers, and another fifth bureaucrats. By 1911 there were also 45,000 students—2,800 of them at Rome University and 8,000 in Rome's many Catholic institutions. As many as 10,000 foreigners were living in the city. At the top of a steeply hierarchical society were those of independent means—papal aristocrats, rentiers, bankers, and other beneficiaries of Rome's expansion. Most women spent their time looking after their families, but they could also find remuneration as domestic servants, prostitutes, lower grade school teachers, and in the occasional white-collar post.

In 1911 the sociologist Domenico Orano published a survey, compiled during the previous five years, of the poor suburb of Testaccio, whose tenements were rising south along the river from the Aventine Hill. Men from this part of town worked either at the new modern municipal abattoir opened in 1891, which now houses the Rome Museum of Contemporary Art, or at the power station on the Viale Ostiense, now the Museo Montemartini. The power station was the brainchild of a reforming municipal administration that took power in 1907 under the Jewish mayor Ernesto Nathan. The Azienda Elettrica Municipale (Municipal Electric Company), which opened in 1909, had nearly 500 consumers in 1912 and more than forty times that number by 1915.

Despite these developments, class and gender divisions yawned in Testaccio. In bourgeois eyes, Testaccio was a coven of criminals, a place where respectable people did not dare to tread. Such prejudice was mistaken, urged Orano, since "the people, in spite of everything, are better than we believe." Living conditions were certainly harsh. Ten people were often crowded into one room, where "adultery, free love, the corruption of minors, and epidemic disease find fertile terrain." Beds stood in kitchens and corridors. As for bathrooms, Orano estimated that many toilets served thirty or more people, and frequently lacked light and water. Abortion was common, and infant mortality rates high; a quarter of children were illegitimate, and half died before their fifth birthday. "Food was often eaten from the same pot wherein it was cooked. One fork and one spoon served the company." All, including the children, drank rough wine, the many taverns acting as "a social safety-valve." It was pointless to deplore the resulting drunkenness and waste of money. The women, Orano pointed out, knew nothing of their own physiology: "Religion is the universal panacea, and it wants nothing to do with clinics, infant schools, or any of the marvelous discoveries of science."

Victims of past and present brutalization, the people of Testaccio were utterly cut off from Roman high culture. Only the "incredible fascination" of the recently introduced cinema offered some relief to "the worker deafened at his factory" or "the illiterate peasant." All rapidly expanding cities are places of high immigration, and Testaccio was no exception. More than half of its inhabitants had not been born in Rome, though these immigrants had not come very far, originating either in the rest of Lazio or in the nearby provinces of Abruzzi, Molise, Marche, or Romagna. In these mean streets, Orano counted only fourteen true foreigners.

On the other side of the city, the San Lorenzo district was little different. In 1907 the educationalist Maria Montessori complained that "the streets are a constant theatre of crime, blood, riot and other foul spectacles, all scarcely to be believed." The area, she said, looked as if it had been devastated by a natural disaster. Crime ruled, and the police were absent. Locals spoke an impenetrable argot, witches still told fortunes, and beggars pursued their age-old and very necessary vocation. A brewery opened in 1902, and a mill and pasta-making enterprise in 1905, offering some employment, as did the nearby Verano cemetery and a garbage dump.

La Marmorata, the main street in Testaccio, with the St. Lazzaro Arch, a painting by Franz Roesler, 1887 (top left); *The Nurse Vittoria* by Grassi, from *Penrose's Pictorial Annual, 1907–1908* (above).

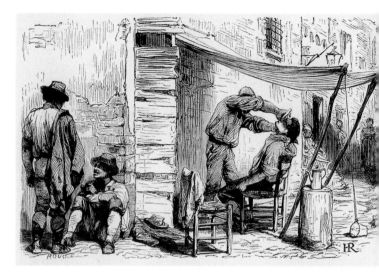

A new church opened in 1909, Chiesa dell'Immacolata San Giovanni, while a restaurant on the corner of Via Latini and Via dei Savelli was known to be a haunt of anarchists. A socialist Chamber of Labor had existed in Rome since 1892, but in 1914 there were still only 1,200 party members in the whole city. To the poor and unemployed of districts like Testaccio and San Lorenzo, religion and politics offered only a distant utopia, and so ironically did the city of Rome. People from such places lived the great part of their lives in their own streets, rarely penetrating the society inside the city walls. There, the comfortable classes, be they Italians or foreign tourists, were aliens from another world.

TRASTEVERE AND TRADITION

Trastevere, west of the river, was considered the more "traditional" area of the city. Augustus Hare typically believed that its residents belonged to "a stronger and more vigorous race" than other Romans, and that something from the classical bloodlines of the city still coursed through their veins. His racial stereotyping convinced him that the Trasteverini committed more murders than did other Romans, thereby expressing their (charming) passion and (picturesque) fondness for wielding a knife. The American novelist Marion Crawford went so far as to maintain that they shared the scalping skills of American Indians. In fact, modernity of some sort was actually reducing crime. Muggings in the city fell from around 350 a year in the 1870s to just sixty-four in 1901; murders fell by a third. Yet in 1908, 160,000 Romans still lived in inadequate housing, while more than 70,000 were indigent. Crawford described Rome as "one of the poorest cities in the civilized world," adding that, while it was "trying to seem rich, the element of sham was enormous in everything."

A 1904 cover from the magazine *Il Socialismo* (top); *Lost Rome*, a painting by Franz Roesler (above); the Trastevere coat of arms (right); an engraving by H. Regnault of an open-air barbershop, from Francis Wey's *Rome* (top right).

Compared with the city's poor, the world of Roman petty bureaucrats and those serving the tourist industry is less well documented. Class was often immediately apparent from men's chins, since the petit bourgeois were accustomed to visit the barber every two or three days, but workers only on Sunday. The historian A. C. Jemolo recorded how food, too, divided the people. Ordinary men and women ate from a bowl held between their knees, their humble fare consisting of bread or a frittata. Petit bourgeois men at lunch, the main meal in a society that still observed siesta, ate two fried eggs (their wives and children one), augmented by vegetables conserved in oil or a lettuce leaf. In winter, this dish would be followed by "some poor quality little apples that would today dishonour the worst fruit vendor of the outer suburbs" or a few chestnuts. At dinner there would be clear soup, a slice of boiled beef, and a vegetable, while on Sunday, *festa* would be marked with a plate of pasta, covered with "a very thick tomato sauce that had a nauseous taste."

RELIGION AND ANTICLERICALISM

In 1905, according to the papal newspaper *L'Osservatore Romano*, 442,394 Catholics, 7,121 Jews, 5,993 Protestants, 312 Orthodox, 38 of other religions, and 2,689 atheists could be counted in Rome. The "liberation" of the city's Jews had been one of the achievements of Rome's Liberal government. Most of the city's ancient ghetto had been rebuilt, and in 1904 a grand new synagogue was opened. King Victor Emmanuel III attended its

A 1900 Anno Santo (Holy Year) postcard (left); Giordano Bruno (right); Ferrari's 1887 statue of Bruno in the Campo dei Fiori.

opening, and expressed his pleasure at the thought that it would be the most important religious edifice to be built in Rome during his reign.

Most Liberals supported the monarch in his anticlericalism. Italy had, after all, been united against the explicit wish of Pope Pius IX. Liberal Italians were now nervously seeking a modern, scientific—and ideally peaceful—global mission for their capital city. One clear expression of the view that modern Rome should overcome the dogma of Catholicism was the inauguration of a monument to Giordano Bruno, who had been burned in 1600 during the counter-reformation for his intellectual independence.

The inauguration of Bruno's statue in the Campo dei Fiori in June 1889 had drawn a vast crowd; the Vatican reacted by closing its gates, summoning into special service a battalion of papal troops, banning any of its workforce from leaving, and accumulating food supplies. Shortly afterward, a ceremony of expiation was held at St. Peter's, and pious foreigners were cordially invited to express their disgust at the intolerable endorsement of heresy in the streets of Rome.

Thereafter, the statue to Bruno was adorned with garlands on September 20 each year, a day set aside in the 1890s as a national holiday, while in February 1900 anticlericals paraded through the Campo dei Fiori as a sign of hostility to the "Holy Year" of 1900—Anno Santo—proclaimed by the pope.

GETTING AROUND

One reason for the relatively meager crowds of that year—only 400,000 people attended the jubilee celebrations—may have been the poor state of the Italian railways, then very much the main way for travelers to reach Rome. The economic and banking crisis of the 1890s had adversely afflicted the railways, which since the Risorgimento had been in the hands of a complex network of private firms. The main lines into Rome were still single track, and trains were notorious for the approximate relationship of their arrivals and departures to any published timetable. In the new decade, reforming governments began to campaign for greater state intervention, Giolitti being particularly anxious that Italian trains should run efficiently and at a profit. After a major strike by railway workers in 1902, pressure increased for decisive action, especially after comparative international statistics placed the Italian railways ahead only of those of Romania and Russia. On April 22, 1905, parliament created the Ferrovie dello Stato under the Ministry of Public Works, formally nationalizing the railway system.

At that time, the motor car was still little seen in the city, and horse-drawn vehicles remained the norm in urban transportation until after World War I. Italy was not without its motoring achievements, however. The 1907 Peking to Paris car race was won by an Italian car, crewed by both the Roman nobleman Prince Scipione Borghese and the Milan-based journalist Luigi Barzini Sr. The actual driving was left to a peasant from one of the Borghese estates. The prince, it was reported, simply showed him the car and told him to drive it.

BUILDING PROGRESS

Back in Rome, the progressive administration of Ernesto Nathan worked hard to improve municipal education, health, and housing—the area around San Saba still stands as a monument to the high standards of the time. As well as bringing the city's energy supplies under public control, the government took public transportation into its hands. On September 20, 1909, a referendum asked Romans to endorse an expanded network of tram tracks for the city; standardized taxi meters had been introduced in 1908. Following a series of debates in 1908 and 1909, Rome developed what many regard as its first real city plan, endeavoring to marry the conservation of its monuments and its inhabitants' need for a better standard of living. An "international exhibition of modern industry" was held in 1909, and in 1911 Nathan demanded a prominent place for Rome in the national fiftieth anniversary celebrations, seeking to unite past and future and to fuse Liberal patriotism with a "modern" mission for the city. During 1911 Rome successively hailed the opening of the new Law Courts, its first modernized racetrack, the German-designed zoo in the Borghese Gardens, and a gallery of

modern art. In addition, an international photography exhibition opened in March of that year; in June came the inauguration of the Victor Emmanuel Monument and a new bridge named for the king, followed by an international archaeological exhibition in the restructured ancient Baths of Diocletian, and an exhibition about Risorgimento history.

SPORT AND THE CITY

In 1911 Rome also saw the opening of the 25,000-seat Stadio Nazionale, designed by the architect Marcello Piacentini, later to become a Fascist notable. A love of soccer was gradually spreading throughout Liberal Italy, though it was largely confined to the northern part of the country. A league had made Juventus of Turin national champions in 1905, but it had only played teams from Milan, Genoa, and Turin. In Rome, Lazio began life in 1900 as a foot-racing club. In 1905 it organized a local soccer tournament, and in 1913 reached the final of the national competition, only to be thrashed 6–0 by a team from Vercelli. The other city team, AS Roma, was founded that same year. Although Italy played its first international match in 1910, winning 6–2 against France, no international games were held as far south as Rome until 1928.

Until the Italian occupation, the most sportive feature of Roman life was an activity known as *pallone con il bracciale*, or "arm-ball." It could draw crowds of 2,000 or more, and much betting and drinking ensued. The Liberals introduced more disciplined games, often with some military training objective. Canoe races on the Tiber began in the 1870s, and a rifle range was opened. From 1884 horse racing was held at Capanelle, a bicycle track opened outside the Porta Salaria in 1894, and in 1910 the Società Ginnastica di Roma was founded under the auspices of Ernesto Nathan and Menotti Garibaldi, son of the famous father. The initiative may have been inspired by rivalry with the church, since in 1908 Pius X had publicly blessed a gymnastic competition at the Vatican.

For visiting Anglo-Saxons, the happiest sporting news of the period was the foundation of the Rome Golf Club in January 1903. A piece of land at Acquasanta—just two miles from the Porta Maggiore, and with views of the Tomb of Cecilia Metella and the Aqueduct of Claudius—was provided for a course by Prince Torlonia, later to be Mussolini's accommodating landlord at the nearby Villa Torlonia. Few Italians were as yet bitten by the golfing bug; the majority of players were foreign, and instruction was given by Scottish professionals.

Ernesto Nathan in 1908 (top);
Pope Pius X, a 1903 inauguration souvenir (bottom).

THE MANY ROMES

On September 20, 1909, Ernesto Nathan expounded his civic ideology in a public meeting at the Porta Pia. The new Rome, he proclaimed, stood essentially for freedom of thought. He mocked Catholic dogma such as papal infallibility—it was, he pronounced, "the reverse of the biblical revelation of the son of God made man on earth, being rather a son of man making himself God on earth." Nathan rejoiced that new state schools were being opened throughout the city. Still more were needed, especially where "churches were in superabundance," and where their obscurantism had not yet been replaced by scientific enlightenment.

Pius X was furious, and publicly denounced such rudeness from a mayor he dismissed as "an exotic and uncivilized Jew." Such a bold attack on "the mission entrusted by Christ to St. Peter and his successors" was not to be tolerated. Entirely unrepentant, Nathan countered that the pope was a reactionary, foolishly waging an antimodernist crusade. Pius was the sworn enemy of "any who searched for a faith that reconciled intellect and heart, tradition and evolution, knowledge and religion," and it was only to be expected that he would oppose a reforming and democratic administration's intention to distinguish between "the Rome of the past and the Rome of the present."

Despite all its good works, however, the Nathan administration collapsed in 1913. Rome would not prove to be an enduringly triumphant center of rational modernity. War and Fascism were in the wings. Perhaps, after all, the city was too complex to don a single history. As Freud would meditate in his *Civilization and Its Discontents* twenty years later, Rome could be seen as "a psychical entity in which nothing that has once come into existence will have passed away, and all the earlier phases of development continue to exist alongside the latest one."

Thus, amid the ruins and the economic growth, Catholics still treasured a holy city with a timeless mission to resist modernization. The futurists condemned Rome as hopelessly bogged down in the past, and imagined freeing the nation from what its leading spokesman called "the leprosy of ruins" through cleansing aerial bombardment and burying what was left in a locked coffin. The Italian avant-garde remained more happily entrenched in Florence, Milan, or even Paris, than in their country's capital, even though their turn-of-the-century anxiety was still heavily nourished by their myth of Rome.

CULTURE AND TOURISM—
AN ENDURING CONUNDRUM

In 1905 as now, opera was one of Italy's cultural glories. In the first decade of the twentieth century, Giacomo Puccini was in his prime, producing *Tosca* in Rome in 1900, *Madama Butterfly* at La Scala in Milan in 1904, and *La Fanciulla del West* (The Girl of the Golden West)—appropriately enough—at the Metropolitan in New York in 1910. Puccini was publically apolitical but in reality a reactionary; as a Tuscan with cosmopolitan range and reputation, he had no special fondness for his nation's capital city. In spite of the stated intentions of their composer, his operas reflected the changing world around him. *Tosca* was anticlerical in its implications; *Madama Butterfly* reminded Europeans of a Japan that was just emerging onto the world stage and which, in 1905, would overcome the might of Russia; and *La Fanciulla del West* was the first operatic spaghetti western, staged as the U.S. economy was racing past

its European competitors, and when massive numbers of Italian emigrants were reaching American shores.

Most people traveling from Italy to America went to stay; most of those going to Rome had a much more limited ambition—to remain long enough to see the sights and buy souvenirs, and then to hasten back to their comfortable homes. The Eternal City had long been part of the Grand Tour for the very rich, but by 1905 it was accessible and affordable to thousands of educated and artistic visitors every year. The tourist industry was well established, and not afraid of so naming itself. Baedeker and Murray sold more copies of their guides to Rome than almost any other destination, and the A&C Black volume for which Alberto Pisa painted the pictures in this book was

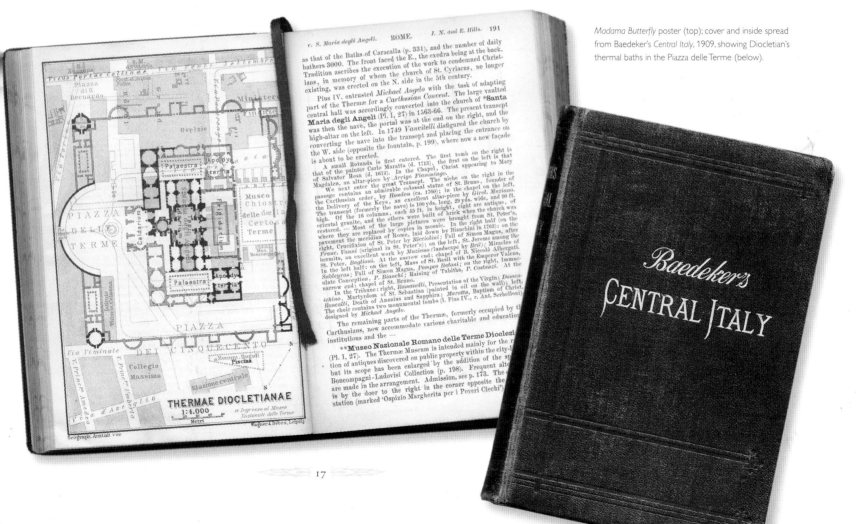

Madama Butterfly poster (top); cover and inside spread from Baedeker's *Central Italy*, 1909, showing Diocletian's thermal baths in the Piazza delle Terme (below).

Hotel Royal stationery with a letter written on December 27, 1904 (above); Rennell Rodd looking suitably stern (middle); *A Silent Greeting* by Lawrence Alma Tadema, painted in 1891—a romantic vision of ancient Rome (bottom right).

similarly popular. Pisa must have been pleased at how many readers loved his soft images of the city's churches and classical sites, as well as his demure portrayals of prettily costumed and well-nourished girls.

Typical of the decade, since 1900 the Milan-based Touring Club Italiano (TCI) had been doing its best to modernize and systematize Italian tourist offerings. The TCI's persevering secretary, Luigi Vittorio Bertarelli, was very much a man of the future in demanding constant and scrupulous review of hotels and restaurants, a graduated set of training courses for waiters, and regular and published opening hours for museums and other tourist attractions. He also requested that accurate records be kept of tourist spending in order to quantify its major contribution to the balance of payments. Bertarelli was anxious to link the TCI with similar bodies that were developing in other European countries in what he optimistically saw as a steady rise in global civilization. He was to be shocked and dismayed by the barbarism of World War I.

No doubt the improvements that Bertarelli was sponsoring were accepted with pleasure by most visiting foreigners, although many shared Augustus Hare's hope of avoiding serious contact with actual Romans. After all, for most foreign visitors Rome was all in the mind—English tourists still tended to assemble around the Piazza di Spagna and avoid what they feared was greasy Italian food by eating at Mrs. Babington's nearby tea rooms. It existed primarily in their recollection of school Latin and its heroes, in their self-consciously aesthetic viewing of Renaissance

and baroque painting and statuary, and in their assumption that, however beautiful or charming the sights and however sunny the weather, Rome's present-day inhabitants were their natural inferiors. At best they could be viewed as citizens of the least of the great powers, at worst as lascivious and fickle, lazy and superstitious. James Rennell Rodd, who was Britain's longest-serving ambassador to Italy from 1908 to 1919, mused uneasily, "A queer place, Rome—so much is not what it seems, so much that seems is not." Like so many observers, he recognized that the city's features, past and present, were too manifold to be reduced to a single image. In 1905, as in 2008, there were plenty of Romes to be seen or ignored, recalled or forgotten, loved or despised.

ALBERTO PISA
1864–1936

Alberto Pisa was born on March 19, 1864, in Ferrara, Italy. The well-known portrait painter Giovanni Boldini had been born in the same house nineteen years earlier—the two later became close friends. His early studies were in Ferrara with Gaetano Domenichini, and he later attended both the Florence and Rome Academies of Fine Arts.

In Florence he joined the Macchiaioli movement, a group of Tuscan painters, active in the second half of the nineteenth century, who painted outdoors in order to capture natural light, shade, and color, thus breaking with the conventions taught by Italian academicians. In many ways they were forerunners of the French Impressionists.

In 1886 Pisa moved to study in Paris for a few months before settling in London, where he lived for nearly thirty years. There he became friends with John Singer Sargent and James McNeill Whistler, and made his mark with a series of rapidly executed watercolors inspired by aspects of life in the city.

Northeasterly view of the cathedral at Cefalù, from *Sicily* by Spenser Musson, A&C Black, 1911.

"Reading," 1908 (top); Church of San Giovanni degli Eremiti, Palermo, from A&C Black's *Sicily* (bottom).

In 1886 Pisa organized a one-man exhibition of eighty-six paintings in London's Bond Street, and his growing reputation as a *vedutista*—a painter of views—earned him regular commissions. Over the next forty years he exhibited widely and prolifically—in Venice, Bologna (1888), Rome and Florence (1889 and 1927), as well as Paris, where he achieved an honorable mention at the Exposition Universelle in 1889. His main market, however, was in London, where the Fine Art Society showed some five hundred of his pictures over more than three decades. He exhibited twenty-five times at the Royal Academy, beginning with a portrait of W. Gridley, Esq., in 1892.

In 1901 a *Times* review referred to Pisa's watercolors of Italian towns as "charming; both in the details of architecture and in general town views he is far beyond the average of the men who paint picturesque Italy." It may have been this review that led to A&C Black's commission for *Rome* in 1904. The paintings of Rome—and some of Umbria—were displayed at the Fine Art Society in October 1905. Reviewing the exhibition, the *Times* said, "Mr. Pisa shows us Rome full of lights and air, and aglow with beautiful colours in stone and trees and flowers."

His later work as an illustrator for A&C Black consisted of *Pompeii* (1910) and *Sicily*, published in 1911. His illustrations were recycled in a number of later books, as was the publisher's usual practice.

Exhibitors' books give his address as 21 Camden Road Studios, from 1892 to 1908; 13 Eversholt Street, Camden Town, in 1909; and Beare Green Post Office, Holmwood, Surrey, in 1912. A further exhibition of sixty paintings in 1913 at the Dudley Galleries in Piccadilly was entitled "Water-Colours of Surrey," and suggests that he moved happily into a rural environment.

He last exhibited in England in 1919, and by 1920 had moved back to Florence without having made his mark in any of the usual genealogical reference sources such as successive British censuses.

Pisa continued to paint watercolor architectural and genre scenes in Florence and Tuscany during the 1920s, and his last exhibition was in 1927. He died in Florence on July 15, 1930.

His paintings can be found in the collections at the National Gallery of Modern Art in Rome, the Palazzo dei Diamanti in Ferrara, and the Bristol City Museum.

Information for these biographical details was largely provided by the *Dizionario Enciclopedico dei Pittori e degli Incisori italiani* and the *Catalogo Bolaffi della Pittura italiana dell'800*.

The Peristyle House (restored) in Pompeii (top left), from A&C Black's *Pompeii* (1910); "Westminster Bridge," c. 1913 (center); La Caldura, Cefalù, from *Sicily* (below); *Lemon Trees, Spring*, from *Sicily* (top right).

PLATE 1

TEMPLE OF SATURN
FROM THE BASILICA JULIA IN THE FORUM

Forgotten for centuries, a renewed interest in the Forum had grown by 1905.

What we think of today as the Roman Forum is, in fact, a conglomeration of several forums, built by successive rulers, each compelled to leave his personal mark on the city. When Rome was founded, the valley between the Capitoline and Palatine hills was nothing more than a swamp, uninhabitable and used only as a burial ground. By 600 the valley had been drained through a massive sewage system, the Cloaca Maxima; the ground had been pounded flat, and it was now the center of a thriving Rome that would remain the capital of the known world for 500 years.

At one end stood the Regia, the palace of the king, and at the other the Comitium, the seat of all political activity. Building continued throughout the era of the republic, and continual restoration and expansion into what we know today as the

Imperial Forum was carried out by Caesar, Vespasian, Augustus, Domitius, Trajan, Tiberius, Septimus Severus, and Maxentius.

During the barbarian invasions of the Middle Ages, the Forum was sacked repeatedly, and reduced to a cow pasture. The real devastation, however, began in the Renaissance, when the remaining relics were pilfered to be used in the building of Christian churches. The great archaeologist Rodolfo Lanciani, who was in charge of all the excavations within the city when this picture was painted, famously wrote that all the sackings of Rome combined did less harm to the Forum than the building of St. Peter's Basilica.

By the time this painting was made, archaeological work in the Forum was intense. In 1905 Christian Hülsen published an account of recent excavations in which he noted, "The results of this last six years exceed in number and in importance, those of all the preceding periods. The area of the Forum has doubled and, more importantly, the explorations did not stop at the level of the Imperial era, but digging further down, revealed ancient monuments of inestimable historic value."

PLATE 2

THE FORUM FROM THE ARCH OF SEPTIMIUS SEVERUS

The modern Via dei Fori Imperiali covers much of what was once the Imperial Forum.

Walking through the Forum today, it is difficult to imagine what it must have been like in 1905. A quarter of a century later, under Mussolini's Fascist government, a wide road was to split the Forum in half. The Via Dell'Impero, known after World War II as the Via dei Fori Imperiali, was Mussolini's idea of a grand boulevard to rival the Champs Élysées in Paris. It connects the Vittoriano monument in Piazza Venezia with the Colosseum in a wide, straight line.

The cost in lost history was inestimable. In order to create a flat, unobstructed surface, a temple at the north end of the Forum and the Meta Sudans fountain near the Colosseum were destroyed.

Whole sections of the Forum, which had been unearthed in the early years of the twentieth century, were filled in and paved over, making further excavations impossible. Mussolini considered relics of the Middle Ages, so beloved by travelers in 1905, to be "filthy and picturesque." He thought nothing of tearing down most of a medieval neighborhood in order to make way for his new boulevard. In May 1938 Mussolini welcomed Hitler to Rome in an open-car procession down the new Via Dell'Impero.

Pisa's painting shows no hint of the heavy traffic that today traverses the Imperial Forum, crossing Rome on Mussolini's great boulevard. Instead, the Forum appears to be an overgrown graveyard of ancient relics, with the Arch of Titus in the distance, and the Palatine Hill rising above it to the right.

PLATE 3

THE FORUM, LOOKING TOWARDS THE CAPITOL

Not all visitors to the Forum were impressed by its awesome history.

For centuries, the Forum was left to the ravages of the elements, and to the pillaging of Renaissance builders who scavenged it for materials. At one point a furnace was set up in the midst of the ancient ruins to reduce the marble relics to lime. Until the middle of the nineteenth century, when the first excavations began, the valley between the Capitoline and Palatine hills, once the seat of power in the civilized world, was a cow pasture known as the *campo vaccino*.

By the turn of the twentieth century, archaeology had become a respected science, and excavations in the Forum had raised the public's awareness of its great historic value. Most visitors were awed to find themselves following the footsteps of Rome's great senators. Not everyone was so impressed, however. In 1906 the Irish writer James Joyce wrote to his brother Stanislaus from Rome, "I must be a very insensible person. Yesterday, I went to see the Forum. I sat down on a stone bench overlooking the ruins. It was hot and sunny. Carriages full of tourists, postcard sellers, medal sellers, photograph sellers. I was so moved that I almost fell asleep and had to rise brusquely. I looked at the stone bench ruefully but it was too hard and the grass near the Colosseum was too far. So I went home sadly. Rome reminds me of a man who lives by exhibiting to travelers his grandmother's corpse."

PLATE 4

MARBLE RELIEF OF THE AMBARVALIA SACRIFICE, IN THE FORUM

The ultimate Roman ritual, the *suovetaurilia*, involved the sacrifice
of the three animals depicted in this bas-relief—a pig, a sheep, and a bull.

Roman rituals usually involved an offering to the gods such as incense, cakes, wine, or branches of laurel. For very important occasions an animal sacrifice was called for, and the entrails were examined. Any impurities or signs of illness were considered inauspicious. If the entrails seemed dubious, another animal was sacrificed, hopefully with better-looking innards.

The festival of the Ambarvalia was held in late May, honoring the goddess Ceres, who looked after growing plants and represented motherly love. The name is a combination of two Latin words— *ambio* (to go around) and *arvum* (the fields), describing the procession that circled the fields three times before the sacrifice took place. While they marched the fields with the animals, the officiating priests recited the *ambarvale carmen*, a prayer asking Ceres to purify the land. Private family ceremonies were held in the countryside, but within Rome there was a great public ceremony, in which citizens who owned farmlands and vineyards participated. The English word "cereal" is derived from the name of this Roman goddess.

During the early years of the twentieth century, there was a great interest in Roman archaeology. The Forum, which had been looted for materials for centuries, was now invaded by archaeologists from Europe, Britain, and the United States, most notably the Englishman Thomas Ashby. After 1910 the Italian government became alarmed at the number of foreigners digging around in its rubble, and restricted excavations to its own archaeologists.

PLATE 5

ST. PETER'S AND CASTEL SANT'ANGELO FROM THE TIBER

Looking toward the Vatican from a bridge that spans the Tiber,
a single vista encompasses nearly fifteen centuries of Roman history.

The Castel Sant'Angelo, originally built as a tomb for the Emperor Hadrian and completed in AD 139, forms a breathtaking contrast to the dome of St. Peter's Basilica, completed centuries later in 1626. The view has inspired countless attempts at capturing it, from the Jean-Baptiste-Camille Corot's great canvas, painted in 1826, to the photos snapped by today's tourists with digital cameras.

In 1853 George Stillman Hillard wrote in *Six Months in Italy*, "A thousand times had I seen it in engravings, and it was with a peculiar feeling, half recognition and half surprise, that I beheld the real group in the smokeless air of a Roman December. The combination is so happy and picturesque that they appear to have arranged themselves for the special benefit of artists, and to be good-naturedly standing, like models to be sketched. They make a picture inevitable."

During the Middle Ages, a secret passageway was constructed between the two buildings, an escape route from the Vatican to the castle fortress in the event of an invasion. In May 1527, during the sack of Rome by the Bourbon forces of Charles V, as the cannon's roar was heard in the papal chambers, Clement VII made a hurried escape through the corridor, disguised by a cloak thrown over his head. The Swiss Guard still hold the keys to the passage gate.

PLATE 6

TEMPLE OF SATURN FROM THE PORTICO OF THE DII CONSENTES

Many of our Christmas traditions stem from the inauguration of this temple on December 17, 498 BC.

Tertullian, a theologian in the early third century, complained, "You will nowadays find more doors of heathens without lamps and laurel-wreaths than of Christians." Decking our homes with evergreen and holly, placing candles in our window, giving gifts, closing schools, and enjoying feasts are all traditions that were adopted by the early Christians from the two-week-long celebration of the Roman god Saturn. In AD 50, Seneca the Younger wrote, "It is now the month of December, when the greatest part of the city is in a bustle. Loose reins are given to public dissipation; everywhere you may hear the sound of great preparations, as if there were some real difference between the days devoted to Saturn and those for transacting business."

Saturn, the god of agriculture, fathered Jupiter, who rebelled against him and cast him out of the heavens. He took refuge with King Janus in Rome, settled at the foot of the Capitoline Hill where his temple stands, and proceeded to teach the Romans how to farm. What we see in this painting is the temple's third incarnation. Because most of the land in the Forum was consecrated, only a temple to Saturn could be built on this spot, and so it was rebuilt three times over, beginning in the fourth century BC. It was used as a state treasury, housing a fund to be used in case of Gallic invasion.

Like the rest of the Forum, the temple was entirely neglected between the Middle Ages and the advent of archaeological study. The excavations were begun by Giuseppe Valadier and completed in 1837. In Pisa's painting we see the remaining eight columns—six in gray granite flanked by two in red.

PLATE 7

A CORNER OF THE FORUM FROM THE BASE OF THE TEMPLE OF SATURN

King Vittorio Emmanuel III was intensely interested in the Forum excavations.

In 1904 Mary Alsop King Waddington wrote to her mother in the United States, "I had a nice, solitary morning in the Forum, with my beloved Italian guidebook, a little English brochure with a map of the principal sites, and occasional conversations with the workmen, of whom there are many, as they are excavating in every direction, and German tourists. The Germans, I must say, are always extremely well up in antiquities, and quite ready to impart their information to others. They are excavating and working here all the time. The King takes a great interest in all that sort of work, and often appears, it seems, early in the morning and unexpectedly, when anything important is going on."

Her description of the scene is as vivid as Pisa's colors. "I found a nice square stone, and sat there lazily taking in the enchanted views on all sides—the Palatine Hill behind me, the Capitol on one side, on the other the three enormous arches of the Temple of Constantine; at my feet the Via Sacra running straight away to the Colosseum, the sky a deep, soft blue, throwing out every line and bit of sculpture on the countless pillars, temples and arches that spring up on all sides. From a height, the Palatine Hill, for instance, the Forum always looks to me like an enormous cemetery—one loses the impression of each separate building or ruin. It might be a street of tombs rather than the busy centre of a great city."

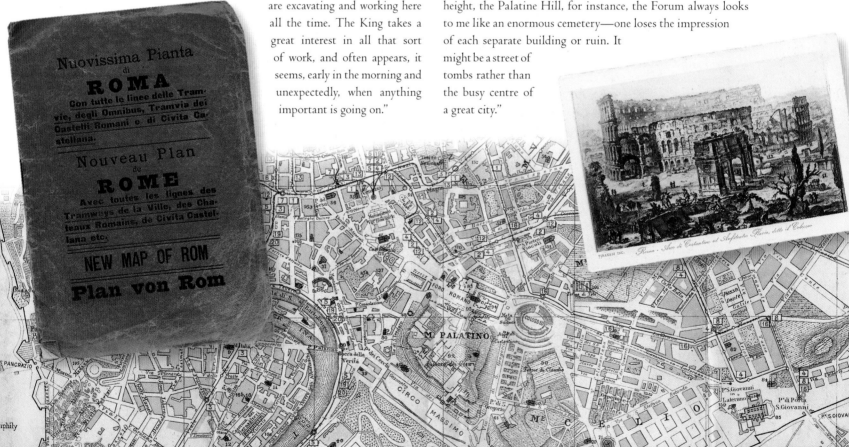

PLATE 8

TEMPLE OF MARS ULTOR

The Temple commemorates the vengeance of Augustus against Caesar's murderers.

The Temple of Mars Ultor (Mars the Vindicator) was built by Emperor Augustus to commemorate his victory at Philippi in Macedonia, where he avenged the death of his adoptive father, Julius Caesar, by slaying two of his assassins, Brutus and Cassius. One of Rome's greatest emperors, Augustus brought a long period of peace to the empire after years of civil war in the wake of Caesar's murder. He also oversaw an enormous amount of building in the capital city.

Suetonius quotes him as claiming that he "found Rome a city of brick and left it a city of marble." Augustus himself boasted that he "built the temple of Mars Ultor on private ground and the forum of Augustus from war-spoils. I built the theater at the temple of Apollo on ground largely bought from private owners, under the name of Marcus Marcellus my son-in-law. I consecrated gifts from war-spoils in the Capitol and in the temple of divine Julius, in the temple of Apollo, in the temple of Vesta, and in the temple of Mars Ultor, which cost me about 100,000,000 sesterces." This was a great deal of money, the equivalent of nearly half of a million U.S. dollars in today's world.

The building of the temple, part of the magnificent Forum of Augustus, began in about 20 BC. Only the eight marble columns remain intact.

The wall with the arched opening we see at the back of the painting was a fireproof barrier protecting the Forum of Augustus from the poor Suburra district behind it, while also serving to block what must have been a rather unpleasant view.

ROMA - Tempio di Marte Ultor

PLATE 9

TEMPLE OF VESPASIAN FROM THE PORTICO OF THE DII CONSENTES

Three Corinthian columns of Carrara marble are all that remain of Vespasian's great temple.

Like many of the great emperors, Vespasian felt the need to leave his mark on the Forum. He was the first of the Flavian dynasty, which followed that of Julius Caesar—a line continued by his sons, Titus and then Domitian. The temple was part of Vespasian's Forum, a great square separated from the forums of Augustus and Caesar. The temple was distinguished by its central area, which was not paved like the other forums but planted as a garden with pools and statues. As it was completed by Domitian in AD 81, after both Vespasian and his son Titus had died, it is often called the Temple of Vespasian and Titus, commemorating them both. Until 1811 it was buried under a layer of rubble and topsoil, later unearthed during excavations by the architect and archaeologist Guiseppe Valadier, who restored it to prevent a total collapse threatened by cracks in the columns.

The church seen behind the arch was originally built by Vespasian and restored by his sons. In 608 Emperor Foca gave the abandoned building to Pope Boniface IV, who remodeled it as a church and dedicated it to Santa Maria and all the Christian martyrs. The arch to the right of the church was built by the Roman senate in 203 in honor of the victories of Septimus Severus and his sons Caracalla and Getus over the Assyrians. Today it looks much the same as it did when Pisa painted it.

PLATE 10

THE COLOSSEUM ON A SPRING DAY

In spring, the flowering trees near the Colosseum are so spectacular that everyone in Rome goes to see them.

The Colosseum, which Mark Twain called "that looped and windowed bandbox with a side bitten out," is the very symbol of Rome. Officially it is called the Anfiteatro Flavio, after the three emperors who built it, all of them members of the Flavian dynasty. The emperor Vespasian began its construction between AD 70 and 80, reclaiming the land from an artificial lake that had been part of the palace of his very unpopular predecessor, Nero. While he was still in power, Nero commissioned a hundred-foot-high gilded bronze statue of himself. Although after his death, Nero's golden palace, the Domus Aurea, was razed to the ground to the cheers of the assembled throngs, the statue remained unharmed, except for its head, which was changed into that of a sun god.

When Vespasian moved it to the entrance of the Colosseum, some reports say that it took twenty-four strong elephants to drag it into place. It remained there for centuries, although the face of the statue was modified to resemble whoever was in power at the time. Eventually, the amphitheater became affectionately known as the Colosseum, after the colossal statue.

Vespasian died before the amphitheater was completed, but his son, Titus, inaugurated it in grand style, with a hundred consecutive days of festivities. It was not fully finished, however, until the reign of Titus's successor, Domitian.

PLATE 11

THE COLOSSEUM AT SUNSET

In 1905 it was fashionable to drive by the Colosseum by moonlight.

At the end of an evening, card tables, after-dinner drinks, and ices were abandoned and the assembled party would crowd into coaches to drive by the Colosseum, lit up by the moon.

In his novel *Daisy Miller*, Henry James's heroine says, "Well, I have seen the colosseum by moonlight … That's one thing I can rave about." James was a great admirer of the monument, using it as a motif in four of his novels. In his travelogue *A Roman Holiday*, he wrote, "One of course never passes the Colosseum without paying it one's respects—without going in under one of the hundred portals and crossing the long oval and sitting down awhile, generally at the foot of the cross in the centre. I always feel, as I do so, as if I were seated in the depths of some Alpine valley."

The Italians are consummate artists when it comes to lighting their monuments, and the Colosseum by night is no less thrilling today, even though the moon is outshone by electric floodlights.

PLATE 12

ARCH OF TITUS

The arch was built to celebrate the Roman victory in Jerusalem.

The Arch of Titus has been used as the model for many triumphal arches erected all over the world. Emperor Domitian dedicated the arch to the memory of his older brother, Titus, who died in AD 81. Eleven years earlier, Titus had returned to Rome victorious, having accomplished the sack of Jerusalem, effectively ending the four-year Jewish war.

Excavations around the arch began in 1904, and had not been completed when this painting was made. While much of the Forum was destroyed during the Middle Ages, the arch endured because it was incorporated into a fortress by the wealthy Roman Frangipane family. It was one of the first of the Forum relics to undergo restoration, which began in 1817 and were continued by the great architect Guiseppe Valadier under Pius VII in 1821. In order to differentiate the new portions from the original arch, Valadier used travertine masonry, new capitals, and a new inscription.

In the sixteenth century, Pope Paul IV, infamous for locking Rome's Jews in a ghetto, forced them to gather each year at the arch to renew an oath of submission. After the ghetto was finally abolished in 1870, Jews refused to walk under the arch in protest against the destruction of the temple in Jerusalem, which it commemorates. In 1948, however, when the state of Israel was founded, a group of Roman Jews gathered at the arch and symbolically walked through it in the opposite direction from that taken by the ancient Roman triumphal march. The carving of the seven-branched chandelier from the Jerusalem Temple, which decorates the arch, was the model for Israel's national coat of arms.

PLATE 13

A PROCESSION IN
THE CATACOMB OF CALLISTUS

Today the catacombs are well-lit and tourist-friendly,
but in 1905 a visit to the underground tombs took some courage.

The miles of tunnels under the city that served as burial places for the early Christians, in some places four levels deep, have excited visitors to Rome for centuries. For a long time they were thought to have been secret meeting and even living places. Mark Twain was among the misguided in this respect; in *The Innocents Abroad* he wrote, "During seventeen years—from 235 to 252—the popes did not appear above ground. Four were raised to the great office during that period. Four years apiece, or thereabouts. It is very suggestive of the unhealthiness of underground graveyards as places of residence."

In fact, no one actually lived in the catacombs. The early Christian burial places were simply replicas of Roman Jewish catacombs. The Romans cremated their dead, while the Jews and Christians buried them. Some accommodation had to be made, and the catacombs provided a way to fit a lot of bodies into a small space. The tunnels are lined with shelves on which the dead were placed, wrapped in two shrouds, with a layer of lime

in between. Estimates vary as to how many miles of catacombs there are on the outskirts of Rome, but those called after St. Calistus, adjacent to the Chiesa di San Sebastiano on the ancient Appian Way, are considered to be the most important.

In 1854 the archaeologist Giovanni Battista de Rossi discovered the crypts of five popes who reigned from 230 to 283, and presented his evidence to Pope Pius IX. Fifty years later, when Pisa painted this image, it was still *the* catacomb to see. Most of the remains of dead Christians had been removed by previous popes and placed in various churches, while others had been smuggled out of the country by a black market in bone trading, which supplied the rest of Europe with its need for relics. But there was still plenty to see—walls covered in inscriptions, religious paintings, and frescoes.

In 1905 the visitor was entirely at the mercy of his monastic guide, who might fall ill, get lost himself, or suddenly go mad. The possibilities for mystery did not escape the great Sir Arthur Conan Doyle, who set his story *The New Catacomb* in the tunnels of St. Calistus. "I had some very narrow escapes at first," one character warns another, "but I have gradually learned to go about. There is a certain system to it, but it is one which a lost man, if he were in the dark, could not possibly find out. Even now I always spin out a ball of string behind me when I am going far into the catacomb."

Palestrina (Cardina) 2/8 905

Cordiali saluti

ROMA
Via Appia veduta S. Sebastiano

No. 176 Ernesto Richter,
Via Serpenti 170,
Editore, Roma.

PLATE 14

FLAVIAN BASILICA ON THE PALATINE

The Palatine Hill was the choicest piece of real estate in ancient Rome.

The Palatine Hill was a favorite place where the rich and the royal built their villas during the heyday of ancient Rome. The hill afforded panoramic views, and it was convenient to the Forum on the flat land just below. None of these villas was more glorious than the Flavian Palace, built by emperor Domitian, the last of the Flavian dynasty. It covered nearly the entire hill, with two wings—one a private residence, the other a more public place, with offices and grand rooms for royal audiences and meetings. The word *basilica*, as it is used here, refers to a meeting place. Christian churches imitated the architecture of these Roman halls, which explains why we have come to think of the word in association with great religious buildings.

The great villa was remodeled by successive occupants, remaining the home of the Roman emperors for some three hundred years. Domitian, who insisted on being called *dominus et deus* (lord and god), built the palace to reflect the might of the emperor. His contemporary, the poet Statius, described it this way: "Awesome and vast is the edifice, distinguished not by a hundred columns but by as many as could shoulder the gods and the sky if Atlas were let off. The Thunderer's palace next door gapes at it and the gods rejoice that you are lodged in a like abode ... so great extends the structure and the sweep of the far-flung hall, more expansive than that of an open plain, embracing much enclosed sky and lesser only than its master."

Roma - Palatino - Il Palazzo dei Flavi

PLATE 15

LIBRARY OF THE HOUSE OF DOMITIAN ON THE PALATINE

Emperor Domitian, a man of letters, included a vast library in his palace complex.

Although historians of the time put Domitian down as one of the "bad" emperors for his despotic behavior, he had his finer points. Under his reign, a great many building projects came to fruition, including three temples deifying members of his family, the Flavia. These were the Temple of Vespasian and Titus, the Porticus Deorum, and the Temple of the Gens Flavia. He also built a great stadium in what is now the Piazza Navona. And then there was his own great palace on the Palatine Hill, known as the House of Domitian, the Flavian Palace or, more properly, the Domus Flavia.

Domitian was a great lover of sport and of the arts. In AD 86 he inaugurated the Capitoline Games, held every four years like the Greek Olympics. The competitions were not just in sports and athletics, but also in oratory, music, and acting. Every year he held a literary competition at his country villa in the Alban Hills, in honor of the goddess Minerva, whom he considered his personal protector.

As he was a man of letters, his library was an impressive and important part of his massive palace complex. All that remains today are the ruins, and a few of the hundreds of columns that adorned the buildings.

PLATE 16

FORUM OF NERVA

During the Middle Ages, this relic was known as Le Colonnacce, "those old columns."

By the time Emperor Nerva came to power in AD 96, there was little available land left in the Forum. During his brief two-year reign, he completed the buildings begun by his predecessor, Vespasian's second son, the tyrannical Domitian.

For his own forum, Nerva had to make do with the narrow strip between the Forum of Caesar and Vespasian's Temple of Peace. Because it connected the two areas, it was also known as the Forum Transitorium.

Little remains of it today. What was left after the ravages of Barbarian invasions and Renaissance pilfering was destroyed under the orders of Pope Paul V, who wanted the marble for his fountain, the Acqua Paola, popularly known today as the *fontanone* (great fountain) on the Janicolo Hill. As if that were not insult enough, Nerva's Forum was cut in half when Mussolini built his Via dell'Impero, the wide boulevard leading from the Piazza Venezia to the Colosseum.

The frieze we see between the two columns represents the goddess Minerva, whom Domitian considered his divine patron.

PLATE 17

FOUNTAIN OF TREVI

Toss a coin in the fountain on your last day in Rome and you're sure to come back.

Since it was completed in 1762, the fountain has attracted ever-increasing hordes of visitors, making it almost unapproachable at busy times. Even at the time of Pisa's painting, it would have been difficult to obtain this unobstructed view.

The fountain has its origins in ancient Rome, when it was customary to build something spectacular to mark the place where water from the aqueducts reached the city. The water in the Trevi is the endpoint of the aqueduct called the Acqua Vergine, because its source, some fourteen miles outside the city, was supposedly discovered in 19 BC with the help of a young girl, who pointed it out to thirsty Roman soldiers. With the sacking of Rome in 537, the aqueducts were all destroyed, leaving Rome without clean water and reducing the people to rely on the Tiber for drinking, washing, and dumping sewage. More than a century later, in 1453, the Renaissance pope Nicholas V restored the aqueduct and commissioned a simple basin at the point where it reached Rome. Three hundred years later, no simple basin would do for the popes of the Baroque. Clemente XII awarded the commission for this monumental "Court of the King of the Oceans" to the winner of a design contest. The winning architect, Nicola Salvi, died at the age of thirty from all the time he spent in the fountain's dampness. The fountain

appears even larger than it really is, because of the smallness of the surrounding square, also called Trevi, from the Italian *tre vie*, which refers to the three streets that come together here.

The Trevi's water is the sweetest in Rome, so delicious that English expatriates used to keep jugs of it in their rooms for making tea. An enormously romantic backdrop, the fountain figures in several nineteenth-century novels and in many films, most notably *Three Coins in the Fountain*, *Roman Holiday*, and *La Dolce Vita*.

In order to be sure you would return to Rome, you used to have to take a sip of the water under the midnight moon. Now it's a lot easier. The current routine is to turn your back to the fountain and toss a coin with your right hand over your left shoulder—any time of day will do. The hundreds of euros that fill the fountain are raked up daily and donated to charity.

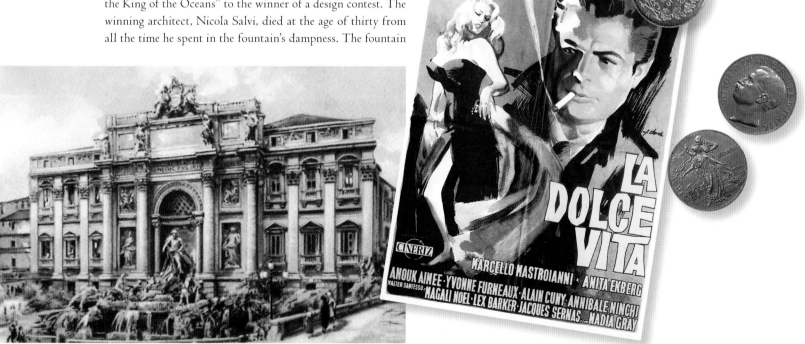

PLATE 18

COLUMN OF MARCUS AURELIUS, PIAZZA COLONNA

At the turn of the twentieth century, the piazza was a
meeting place with open-air cafés and frequent concerts.

In 1905 it was common to take one's open carriage for a spin up the Via del Corso toward the Piazza del Popolo and the Borghese Gardens, stopping at the Colonna to greet one's similarly occupied friends and acquaintances. The column, which gives the piazza its name, was erected by—and in honor of—Marcus Aurelius in the second century, a celebration of the philosopher-emperor's victories over the unwashed hordes from the north. The story of his glory winds its way around the column in a rather crude relief, copied from the column that Emperor Trajan had had erected to himself a century earlier.

The statue of St. Paul, which tops the column, replaces an earlier one of Marcus Aurelius, which was lost during the Middle Ages.

Olave Potter described the column in her 1909 book, *The Colour of Rome*: "Its marble is stained and mellowed by time, and the twisted script is being slowly obliterated." In fact, the column continued to deteriorate until it was cleaned up for the jubilee year of 2000.

In the time of the Roman Empire, the square also contained a temple to Marcus Aurelius and a crematorium. By the turn of the twentieth century, these had already been replaced by the Widekind and Chigi palaces, today respectively the offices of the right-wing newspaper *Il Tempo* and of Rome's national government.

Writers and artists frequented a café at the edge of the square, the Caffé Aragno. At about the time of Pisa's painting, these would have included James Joyce, Oscar Wilde, and Émile Zola.

PLATE 19

PANTHEON, A FLANK VIEW

Until the middle of the nineteenth century, the great Pantheon was
immersed in squalor, its noble portico the scene of a poultry market.

The poultry market had gone by 1905, but the square was no less colorful, the scene of a steady stream of pilgrims and tourists. No one comes to Rome without visiting the Pantheon. H. V. Morton wrote in *A Traveller in Rome*, "You may spend days in the Forum trying to imagine what Rome was like in the days of its imperial greatness, but the Pantheon remains the only visible evidence." It is the only building to have survived the centuries intact, although much of its decoration has been removed. In 633 Emperor Constans took the gilded roof tiles in order to use them in Constantinople, and in 1625 Pope Urban VIII Barberini made eighty guns for Castel Sant'Angelo from the bronze of the porch ceiling.

Originally built in 27 BC by Agrippa, as the engraving on the portico proudly proclaims, it was rebuilt by the more modest Emperor Hadrian between AD 118 and 125, and it is generally considered that Hadrian himself was the genius who conceived its architecture. If the great dome of St. Peter's Basilica were laid on the ground, it would just fit inside the dome of the Pantheon, which until the twentieth century was the largest dome in the world.

The building fell into disrepair in the Middle Ages, but in 605 the Byzantine emperor Foca ceded it to Pope Boniface VIII, thereby saving it for posterity. The pope promptly replaced the Pantheon of pagan gods with Christian martyrs, and reconsecrated the building as the Basilica di Santa Maria ad Martyres. It is the burial place of the great painter Raphael and of the first kings of united Italy—Vittorio Emmanuelle II and Umberto I.

Pisa has chosen an interesting view of the Pantheon, painting it from the flank, so that the rounded walls of the dome are visible as well as the columned portico. The black-clad figures seen parading by are members of the Confraternity of St. John the Beheaded, a group founded in the thirteenth century, whose duty it was to administer to criminals condemned to death.

PLATE 20

SILVERSMITHS' ARCH IN THE VELABRUM

The Velabrum, once a marshy swamp, became one of the busiest areas in the Roman Forum.

During the time of the Roman Empire, the Velabrum was a busy marketplace beside the Tiber. Its ancient name refers to the marshy swamp where, according to legend, Faustolus found the twins Romulus and Remus floating in a basket that had become stuck in the roots of a fig tree.

When the great drainage sewer, the Cloaca Maxima, was built, the land was reclaimed and became a part of the Forum. The arch, incorrectly translated here as the silversmiths', was actually built by the guild of money changers and cattle merchants who traded in the Forum Boarium, the *argentari et negotiantes boari*. It was erected in 204 in honor of Emperor Settimo

Severo and his wife Giulia Domna, who are represented in the reliefs on the cornice. Originally there were also reliefs and inscriptions to the couple's son Geta, his wife Plautilla, and his father-in-law Plautianus. After Geta's brother, Emperor Caracalla, had them all murdered, he had their names and likenesses removed from the arch.

The holes in the arch were probably made by medieval treasure hunters who imagined that the money changers had hidden their gold within the fabric of the structure.

PLATE 21

CONVENT GARDEN OF SAN COSIMATO, VICOVARO

Today the monks host weddings and conventions in these beautiful gardens.

The Sabine Hills, an hour or so by car from Rome, have been a popular retreat since the days of ancient Rome, when those who could afford it escaped the summer heat by fleeing to higher elevations. The poet Horace kept a farm there, and during the Middle Ages numerous convents were erected along the hilltops.

The convent of St. Cosimato was established in the sixth century. Like other monasteries in the region, it was destroyed by the Saracen invasion and rebuilt several times. The Franciscan brothers moved into the convent in 1648, only to have it confiscated by the state in 1876 after the unification of Italy. When this picture was painted, the convent was being used as a hospital.

Pisa must have been struck by the medieval bell tower, which he cleverly placed in the background, choosing not to paint the Renaissance and Baroque aspects added during the course of many restorations and renovations. Mussolini returned the convent to the Franciscan brothers in 1936. They have recently opened a hostel and retreat center, hosting scout groups, weddings, and meetings, with a shuttle bus connecting the convent with the center of Rome.

PLATE 22

A TRACT OF THE CLAUDIAN AQUEDUCT OUTSIDE THE CITY

The remains of the great aqueducts still stand like architectural dinosaurs
in the midst of the Roman countryside.

The nine aqueducts that brought water to Rome from lakes and springs in outlying areas are one of the engineering wonders of the ancient world. Without them, the city would never have become the great international capital it was.

The Claudian Aqueduct, built by Emperor Claudius in the first century AD, was surely the most grand of the nine in terms of the architecture, running for six miles, with arches as high as 109 feet. It was engineered using mostly simple gravity feed, with a little help from the occasional pump house, and some seven hundred engineers were employed to maintain the continuous slope of the aqueducts. When they finally reached the city,

the waters of the Claudian Aqueduct spilled into a fountain at the foot of the Palatine Hill. From there, it was distributed to the home of the emperor and to rich Romans who could afford the price of indoor plumbing.

A great amount of water was used to supply the public bath complexes. For the plebeians, there were plenty of public fountains, never more than a hundred feet apart, from which they could take water for household use. Today, as in 1905, the remains of these great water channels are among the most striking features of the Roman countryside.

Campagna Romana · Verso il pascolo.

PLATE 23

CAMPAGNA ROMANA, FROM TIVOLI

Idyllic scenes like this can still be found not far from the bustle of Rome.

In 1905 a short walk through one of the gates in the old Aurelian walls would take you straight into an agricultural landscape, with grazing sheep and cows and rolling greenery. Today the city's sprawl has infringed on all that.

Soon after the reunification of Italy, when Rome became the capital of the newly formed country, suburbs began to spring up. The first expansion was to the north, which is now a lovely neighborhood of Liberty-style apartment buildings, dating from the late nineteenth and early twentieth centuries.

After World War II, during the boom years of *La Dolce Vita* as the country began to rebuild itself, blocks of apartments took over the former countryside, and entire new neighborhoods appeared. Quickly constructed and with little charm, this urban periphery has continued to expand all the way to the airport at Fiumicino, stretching out in every direction.

Today a drive to Tivoli, for example, takes only an hour or so along modern highways that pass by shopping malls and car lots. The medieval hilltop town has, however, lost only a little of its magic, and it is still possible to find scenes like the one Pisa painted more than a century ago.

PLATE 24

SUBIACO FROM THE MONASTERY OF ST. BENEDICT

This ancient monastery is carved into the side of a rocky mountain.

Even with today's excellent highways, a visit to Subiaco, forty-eight miles east from Rome, can mean a two-hour drive. In 1905 the trip would have taken all day, traveling by horse and carriage on country roads that wound up the mountainside.

But for an artist in search of a subject, it was clearly worth it. Pisa painted several pictures of the magnificent landscape and the monastery's Gothic architecture. St. Benedict established the order in this region, founding thirteen monasteries in the Simbruini mountains, each with a community of twelve brothers and a superior.

Today, only a handful of monks reside in two monasteries at Subiaco—Santa Scholastica, which we see in this painting, and San Benedetto, less than a mile above it, where the artist would have set up his easel.

Sadly, more than three quarters of Subiaco was destroyed during an American bombardment of German positions in 1944. The Monastery of San Benedetto, built directly into the rocks, was largely spared, but Santa Scholastica below it suffered severe damage, and was not fully restored until 1994.

PLATE 25

GARDEN OF THE MONASTERY OF SANTA SCHOLASTICA, SUBIACO

The monastery has been continuously inhabited by the Benedictine order for 1,400 years.

This little garden was designed as both a place for reflective prayer and mediation, and as a practical place for the cultivation of herbs, which the monks still use in the making of tisanes and liquors. Symbolically, the garden represents the Garden of Eden, while the well represents God, the source of all living things.

Founded in the seventh century, Santa Scholastica is the oldest Benedictine monastery in the world, continuously inhabited by monks for more than fourteen centuries. Scholastica, St. Benedict's sister, preceded him in his vocation, becoming a nun before he devoted himself to a life of prayer. The monastery was dedicated to her by Pope Benedict VII in the tenth century.

In addition to the three traditional vows of chastity, poverty, and obedience, Benedictine monks take a fourth vow of stability. As he makes his final commitment to the order, each brother is asked to choose a monastery that will become his home for the rest of his life. Today, sixteen monks live out their days at Santa Scholastica, and four at the monastery of San Benedetto, just above it on the same mountainous site. The brothers maintain a small hostel on the grounds, with sixty beds for travelers, conventions, and school groups; there is also a restaurant and meeting rooms.

PLATE 26

HOLY STAIRS AT THE SACRO SPECO

These steps connect the middle and upper chapels of the isolated monastery.

The *sacro speco*, the sacred grotto, refers to the small cave in the mountains above the town of Subiaco where St. Benedict lived in total isolation for three years. In the twelfth and thirteenth centuries, an exquisite monastery was built over the grotto where Benedict lived. Carved into the rocky side of Mount Talèo, it is in the Gothic style.

The painting gives us a glimpse of the magnificent frescoes and mosaics that virtually cover the monastery's interior walls and ceilings, and the interlocking Gothic arches and vaults that are used throughout. All of the frescoes in this part of the church were painted in the twelfth century by the same unknown artist. They give the supplicant a great deal to contemplate while slowly ascending step by step from Our Lady's Chapel to the Chapel of St. Gregory. The most impressive fresco depicts death as a long-haired skeleton with black eyes, riding a galloping stallion as he strikes a young man.

Today, groups of visitors touring the monastery are led quickly down these stairs by an Italian guide, but one could spend months contemplating their detail and symbolism without fully appreciating their great wealth of imagery.

PLATE 27

LITTLE GLEANER IN THE CAMPAGNA

This small girl was sent to gather the wheat that remained on the ground after the harvest.

The poverty of many farm workers made gleaning essential to survival. This girl, walking barefoot on a road above one of the hillside towns that dot the Roman countryside, has been gleaning the wheat left on the ground after the harvest. Until the reunification of Italy in 1870, farming remained an almost feudal operation. Nobles owned huge tracts of land that were worked by their peasants. The *padrone*, or owner, was almost like a father figure to these families. Even after reunification, when Italy became a republic, the parliament was controlled by the large landowners, and universal suffrage was still decades away.

Despite the power of the landowners, common land and ecclesiastical estates began to be sold off in small parcels, creating an agrarian middle class, particularly in the rural areas just outside Rome, which had formerly been part of the Papal States. The most common crop in central Italy was wheat,

but in the early 1880s, when wheat prices fell by a third, the small farms began to collapse. Landowning peasants, unable to meet mortgage and tax payments, were forced off their farms, contributing to the mass exodus of Italians to the United States, Argentina, and Brazil.

PLATE 28

SEA HORSE FOUNTAIN
IN THE VILLA BORGHESE

During the eighteenth century, the Borghese Gardens were remodeled in the English style.

The Fontana dei Cavalli Marini, known as the "sea horse fountain," is one of fifteen major fountains in Villa Borghese. Like most of the others, this one was added in the eighteenth century, when the grounds were transformed from their original Baroque design to resemble something similar to an English garden, with the addition of many ornamental fountains and statues. In the painting, which appears to have been made at twilight, it is hard to see the fountain's main feature, a circle of horses at the base. These are full-sized, four-legged horses in the sea, as opposed to the little hook-shaped creatures we call "sea horses." The fountain, once thought to be the work of the great Renaissance artist Gian Lorenzo Bernini, was, in fact, made centuries later by the Tyrolean painter Cristoforo Unterberger and carved by sculptor Vincenzo Pacetti, who was busy with a good many of the decorations added to the gardens at that time.

PLATE 29

ORNAMENTAL WATER, VILLA BORGHESE

The gardens had been a public park for only two years when Pisa made this painting.

This artificial lake was added to the gardens in the late eighteenth century by Prince Marcantonio Borghese IV. The temple, strategically placed to reflect in the waters, is an imitation of a Greek temple to the god of medicine, Aesculapius. It was designed in the Ionic style by Antonio and Mario Asprucci, with the collaboration of the Tyrolean sculptor Cristoforo Unterberger.

Elsewhere in the gardens, a fountain dedicated to the same god boasts an original Roman statue from the classic period.

Since the gardens became a public park in 1903, the lake has been the romantic backdrop for lovers, a place for children to sail toy boats and for dogs to cavort. On a sunny summer's day all three will usually be found there, along with the ducks we see swimming placidly in Pisa's painting.

PLATE 30

VILLAGE STREET AT ANTICOLI, IN THE SABINE HILLS

In 1905 Anticoli was well known as a village of artists and models.

In the eighteenth century, the sleepy mountain town of Anticoli was discovered by many of the artists who flocked to Rome from northern Europe and Great Britain. At that time, and for decades afterward, young women waited on Rome's Spanish Steps in the hopes of being hired as artists' models. Many of the most beautiful were from Anticoli, and eventually the artists became curious about a village that could produce so many lovely young women.

Even today the town is not easily reached from Rome, perched as it is on the side of a steep hill, up a winding road, more than thirty miles from the city. Then as now, however, those who made their way to the village were enchanted. It seemed untouched by time, and the views of the surrounding mountains and the valley below, with the Aniene River flowing through it, were breathtaking.

Today the population of Anticoli is a scant 900, but in 1905 it was twice that size, owing in no small part to the artists who transformed crumbling country houses into studios, often marrying their models and settling down in the village. Among the famous artists and writers who lived here are the artist Oskar Kokoschka and the playwright Luigi Pirandello. Scores of lesser-known artists painted hundreds of pictures in and around Anticoli, and in 1935 a museum was established in the village to exhibit them.

PLATE 31

VILLA D'ESTE, TIVOLI

Cardinal Ippolito d'Este spent the last twenty years of his life creating this astonishing villa.

Tivoli has been a summer retreat since the days of the Roman republic. Its hilltop position makes for a cooler climate, and the sulfur-rich natural springs, which give off an odor noticeable even from the highway, have been an attraction since ancient times.

Emperor Hadrian built an immense villa and gardens at Tivoli that has today become an archaeological park. For centuries, the rich and powerful continued to build villas at Tivoli, but the Villa d'Este is a wonderland like no other, with elaborate terraced water gardens that have earned it a place in UNESCO's list of World Heritage Sites. It was built in the sixteenth century by Cardinal Ippolito d'Este, who was the son of Lucrezia Borgia and the Duke of Ferrara. His grandfather, Pope Alexander VI, made him a bishop when he was only two years old, paving the way for his quick rise through the church hierarchy. He might have been made pope, but a jealous Julius III made him governor of Tivoli—in effect exiling him from Rome.

To console himself, he spent the last twenty years of his life building the magical villa, covering the walls and ceilings with frescoes in the grotesque style, and creating one of the most astounding water gardens in the world.

PLATE 32

IN VILLA BORGHESE

Cardinal Scipione Borghese created one of the greatest Baroque gardens in the world.

In 1605 Cardinal Scipione Borghese—nephew of the famously nepotistic Pope Paolo V and one of the greatest collectors of art the world has ever known—began buying up the wooded land and vineyards just beyond Rome's city walls in order to build a "casino" to serve as a showcase for his collection and a place to entertain. He gradually acquired a 148-acre heart-shaped property and, with the help of landscape architect Domenico Savini, began the task of re-creating a great Roman garden such as the one designed by Emperor Hadrian for his villa at Tivoli. The garden, divided into three principal areas to accommodate the shape of the property, had formal Baroque elements as well as wilderness, and enclosures for exotic animals and birds.

In 1766 the cardinal's descendant, Prince Marcantonio Borghese IV, hired a Scottish artist, Jacob More, to remodel the grounds in the English style, and this is the garden we see in Pisa's painting. The dappled light, coming through the trees, suggests that the picture was made in the spring. In the distance we can see two small figures deep in conversation. The figure in black is a priest, while the one in red is one of the Austrian seminarists, whose costumes earned them the nickname "red prawns."

PLATE 33

THE SPANISH STEPS, PIAZZA DI SPAGNA

The triple staircase of the Spanish Steps refers to the Holy Trinity, and the Trinità dei Monti church at the top.

The "Spanish Steps," as they are known in English, are more properly called the Scalinata di Trinità dei Monti. In fact, they are not Spanish at all but were conceived by one Frenchman and funded by another.

Until they were built in 1726, only a trail led up the steep, tree-covered hill from the piazza below to the French church and convent, the Trinità dei Monti, at the summit. The hilltop was a French enclave of sorts, with the French Academy, formerly the Villa Medici, adjoining the church. The piazza takes its name from the Bourbon Spanish Embassy to the Holy See, which is still there today. The money for the steps, a sum of some 20,000 scudi, was bequeathed by the French diplomat Étienne Gueffier.

In the nineteenth century, the square was so infested by English expatriates that the locals called it the "English ghetto."

A remnant of this foreign occupation can still be seen in Babington's Tea Rooms, to the left of the steps, opened in 1893 by a genteel English lady, and little changed today. To the right is the house where the poet John Keats spent his last miserable months in 1821, dying of tuberculosis and gazing out his window at the stairs. Today it is preserved as the Keats-Shelley Memorial House. In the time of Charles Dickens, the steps served as a showcase for loitering models, whom he described as "mightily amusing," dressed in their picturesque costumes, hoping to be hired by some aspiring English painter. Today, the steps are crowded with loiterers of another sort, Italian teenagers who use the steps as a place to meet and hang out.

4073 ROME - House where Keats lived

PLATE 34

AT THE FOOT OF THE SPANISH STEPS, PIAZZA DI SPAGNA, ON A WET DAY

For many years the foot of this famous staircase was awash with the brilliant colors of flower sellers' stalls.

From the end of the nineteenth century, indeed until recently, the foot of the Spanish Steps was crowded with flower sellers, who could refresh their wares at the nearby fountain, La Barcaccia.

In February 1904, an American woman, Mary King Waddington, widow of the former French premier and ambassador to the Court of St. James, wrote to a friend, "The Spanish Steps looked beautiful, glowing with colour—pink, yellow and that soft grey tint that the Roman stones take in the sunlight. All the lower steps are covered with flower stalls (they are not allowed any longer scattered all over the piazza), and most picturesque they looked—daffodil, mimosa, and peach-blossoms which were very effective."

Today, the flower stalls are gone, but each year in May, the steps are all but covered with pots of pink and white azaleas, and flowering pots hang from lampposts in the neighboring streets.

PLATE 35

ROMAN PEASANT CARRYING COPPER WATER POT

Until the Mussolini era, many Roman homes were without running water.

It was quite usual for a working-class family to get their daily water supply from one of the many public fountains. The most common of these are called *nasone*, meaning "big nose," because of the curved shape of the spout. A jug was placed under the spout to be filled, but a finger placed over the opening would turn the spout into a drinking fountain, thanks to a little hole placed at the top.

Many of these nasone are still operating in Rome's historic center, where tourists use them to refill their water bottles, while the locals use them to rinse their hands or a piece of fruit.

The quality of Rome's drinking water rates near the top of that of the world's major cities, and it is in abundant supply, feeding the city's legendary fountains. Until the twentieth century, most of it still came from the old Roman aqueducts, modernized and repaired through the centuries.

PLATE 36

CHAPEL OF THE PASSION IN THE CHURCH OF SAN CLEMENTE

This lovely chapel was painted during Rome's artistic revival, near the end of the Middle Ages.

Pisa painted a tranquil scene of women in prayer before what appears to be an enormous chapel. In fact, St. Catherine's, as it is called today, is the size of a large closet, inside a small but very important and ancient church, which has been under the auspice of the Irish Dominicans for centuries. Such a scene would be unlikely today, as the church is almost always mobbed with visitors who come to see the excavations of a more ancient church below, but always begin their visit by crowding around this little chapel to hear the guide's lecture.

The saint whose memory and blessed works it honors is St. Catherine of Alexandria, not to be confused with the better-known St. Catherine of Siena. This Catherine was an incredibly persuasive woman. The chapel's beautiful frescoes tell her story, which begins with her successfully arguing with fifty learned men, summoned by the emperor, all of whom she quickly converts to Christianity. The enraged emperor orders that Catherine be burned at the stake, yet she escapes this fate when the empress comes to visit her in prison, and is also converted. The emperor orders an even more painful death, decreeing that Catherine be torn apart between two wheels. She is tied and ready to die when angels appear to release her. Finally the emperor decides to behead her, thinking that surely this should work. Yet miraculously Mount Sinai rises behind her executioner and angels carry her body to the mountaintop, while another angel carries her soul to heaven.

The frescoes have been attributed to an important fifteenth-century painter, Masolino da Panicale, one of the first artists to begin work after the long, dark seventy-year period during which the popes retreated to Avignon, France. They were painted in 1428–1431, during the great artistic revival that began after the return of the papacy.

PLATE 37

A RUSTIC DWELLING IN THE ROMAN CAMPAGNA

Today these humble farmworkers' houses have become luxurious summer residences.

In 1905 these rustic houses in the countryside near the city of Rome were still occupied by farmworkers. Typically, the living space was a short flight of stone stairs up from the ground, the ground level being used to keep poultry or perhaps a goat. Raising the house in this way kept it free of mud in the rainy seasons and from dust in the dry ones. The foliage, which was allowed to invade the roofs and terraces, gave the houses much of their charm.

Houses like this one that have survived the hundred years since this scene was painted have usually been completely remodeled and modernized—now they come with swimming pools, satellite dishes, and large garages. They are the country homes of wealthy Rome residents, and the Italian dream houses of American and British expatriates.

Those houses that have crumbled beyond hope of restoration are often pillaged for the old bricks, which are recycled into new homes with that desirable "campagna" look treasured by Italians and foreigners alike.

Costume della Campagna Romana

PLATE 38

PROCESSION WITH THE HOST AT SUBIACO

The monastery tower seems to dominate the mountainside.

The procession moves up the mountain trail from the Monastery of Santa Scholastica, which we see in the background, toward the Monastery of San Benedetto, less than a mile above it, the site of the grotto where Benedict spent three years in solitary prayer and reflection. It was probably painted on his feast day, March 21, when twilight would have come near the end of the working day.

The tower that rises above the monastery at the back of the procession was built in 1052. It is the oldest part of the complex, which was destroyed and rebuilt many times during the fourteen centuries since it was founded. The medieval tower, said to be the tallest in central Italy, dominates the mountainside. The decorations on the top two rows were added during repairs in the thirteenth and fourteenth centuries.

In 1904 the architect Gustavo Giovannoni wrote that the bell tower is "still standing, like a great, old oak tree, surviving in a forest that has been destroyed. Like a sentinel, it watches over the valley where it has seen so much water pass and witnessed such inconstancy."

PLATE 39

GIRL SELLING BIRDS
IN THE VIA DEL CAMPIDOGLIO

In 1905 the area around the Campidoglio was full of street vendors.

The Via del Campidoglio, today a steep, narrow street, was once the Clivus Capitolinus, part of the route taken by triumphant armies as they proceeded through the Forum and up to the top of the Capitoline Hill, where stood the great temple of Jupiter. The Capitolinus, which became the Campidolgio in Italian dialect, had also been the center of ancient Rome's religious activity.

By the Middle Ages the temples were gone, and a series of palaces took their place. Michelangelo Buonarroti was commissioned by Pope Paul III to create a magnificent square for the visit of King Charles V of Spain, the Holy Roman Emperor, who was expected in 1538. Michelangelo's design is one of the most astonishing architectural works of the Renaissance. He changed the direction of the square so that it faced away from the Forum and toward the Vatican, signaling the new Rome. The square became the seat of Rome's civic government, and Rome's city hall is housed there to this day.

Until 1869, when it was moved to the Campo de'Fiori, the Campidoglio was the scene of a lively open market that spilled onto the neighboring streets, and included the stalls and shops set up in the arches of the nearby Theater of Marcellus. This girl would have been one among many street vendors, selling everything imaginable, from spices to iron tools, souvenirs to cut flowers. Note her costume, typical of girls of her station at the time, with her apron, shawl, and head covering.

PLATE 40

ENTRANCE TO ARA COELI
FROM THE FORUM

The Ara Coeli, the "altar of the heavens," was originally built by Emperor Augustus.

According to Rome's first guidebook, the *Mirabilia Urbis Romae*, written for travelers in the twelfth century, Emperor Caesar Octavian Augustus was horrified to learn that the senate planned to honor him as a god. Feeling unworthy of deification, and afraid that so audacious a move would infuriate the aristocracy, he consulted the Tiburtine Sibyl. She advised him to fast and pray for three days, after which she made the following prophesy: "The signs are clear that justice will be done, and soon the King of the Ages will descend from the sky." Awestruck, the emperor saw a dazzling light with a woman standing on an altar holding a baby in her arms, and he heard a voice proclaiming, "This is the altar of the son of God." So the emperor raised an altar— the Ara Coeli—on the Capitoline Hill.

This may or may not be a true story, but the official church brochure records it as fact, and one of the marble columns inside bears an inscription identifying its source as the emperor's bedroom. Jesus was born during this emperor's reign, which may give further credence to the tale.

By 574 the Ara Coeli was the site of a Byzantine monastery, and in 1249 the pope turned the buildings over to the Franciscans, who remodeled the church in a Romanesque-Gothic style. During the Middle Ages, meetings of the church elders were held at the church, and city politics was discussed there. Today the city is still run from Rome's municipal headquarters, situated just a few yards away on the Capitoline Hill.

PLATE 41

IN THE CHURCH OF ARA COELI

A woman in the colorful dress of the Roman campagna
dips a prayerful hand into the holy water.

A series of mismatched columns, scavenged from ancient Roman ruins, support the three naves of this ancient church. Charles Dickens, in *Postcards from Italy*, called it a "long vista of gloomy pillars." Most visitors have a less jaded reaction, and the church, like so many in Rome, is filled with art treasures, among them frescoes of the life of Saint Bernard of Sienna painted in the fifteenth century by Pinturicchio, tombs sculpted by Donatello and by Michelangelo, a magnificent mosaic floor, and a gilded ceiling that celebrates the sixteenth-century defeat of the Turkish fleet in the Mediterranean.

The church is perhaps best known among Romans for the *bambino*, a life-size wooden sculpture of the baby Jesus. It is said that the original was carved in fifteenth-century Jerusalem by a Franciscan friar, using wood from an olive tree in the Garden of Gethsemane. Over the years, the statue was adorned with jewels by grateful believers, and so was kept behind lock and key, though it was taken out and driven through the town to the bedside of the ill and dying, where its presence was believed to have resulted in miraculous cures. For this purpose the people of Rome donated a carriage for the bambino's personal use. Dickens described the bambino thus: "In face very much like General Tom Thumb, the American dwarf: gorgeously dressed in satin and gold lace and actually blazing with rich jewels." Unfortunately, the statue was stolen in 1995, probably due to its ostentatious display of jewelry. The figure on display at the church today is a perfect reproduction.

PLATE 42

DOORWAY OF THE MONASTERY OF ST. BENEDICT (SAGRO SPECO) AT SUBIACO

An exquisite monastery built into a mountainside commemorates the cave where
St. Benedict lived for three years in solitude.

Benedict was born around 480 to a wealthy Umbrian family. As a young man, he was sent to Rome to complete his studies in order to become a lawyer. The corruption and decadence of the city appalled him to such an extent that he ultimately took refuge in a mountain cave, spending years in lonely prayer and meditation. He was kept alive by a loyal monk, who took what he could from his own meager rations and lowered them with a rope and basket from a cliff high above Benedict's cave. Benedict became one of the great saints of the Middle Ages, founding an order that ultimately spread Christianity throughout Europe.

The door we see in the painting opens onto what is called the "lower church," as the building was carved on several levels into the mountainside. Visitors still enter the monastery here, although today the entrance is preceded by convenient public bathrooms and a room with vending machines selling snacks. None of this ultimately detracts from the effect of the rooms themselves, which are breathtaking in their design and decoration, nor from the monastery's location atop Mount Talèo, which still seems so wild and uninhabited that it is hard to remember that there is a large town just below it.

PLATE 43

CHAPEL OF SAN LORENZO LORICATO AT ST. BENEDICT'S, SUBIACO

The interior of the monastery of St. Benedict is covered with frescoes and mosaics.

Lorenzo Loricato died in 1243. Having accidentally killed a man when he was young, he spent the rest of his life in severe penitence, retreating—like St. Benedict—to a mountain cave. Benedict, who lived for three years in a grotto, inspired generations of the faithful to do likewise, and for several centuries after his death there were always three or four hermit monks living in the caves near the site of the present monastery.

The monastery was built into the side of Mount Talèo, high above the town of Subiaco, over several centuries. The lowest level of the building contains the actual grotto where the saint lived as a hermit. It is now a shrine, with a statue of the saint in prayer staring at a cross.

Pisa's painting gives us an idea of the magnificence of the monastery's frescoed walls and ceilings, and its inlaid marble floors. The arch above the chapel depicts the baptism of Christ, the work of an unknown artist of the School of Siena. This chapel where San Lorenzo Loricato is enshrined is actually called the Chapel of Our Lady. The saint is buried low in one of the walls, adorned with a painting of him in death. Frescoes to the side of the tomb depict scenes from his life.

PLATE 44

STEPS OF THE DOMINICAN NUNS' CHURCH OF SAINTS DOMENICO AND SISTO

This double flight of steps, joining at the top to form a terrace,
may have inspired the Spanish Steps built a century later.

This staircase is as close as Pisa came to painting an example of the Roman Baroque, which was much discredited at the time. Note the friar's dark cloak and hat, garments still worn by the order today, which have earned them the sobriquet "Black Friars."

The church was begun in the middle of the sixteenth century on the order of Pius V, himself a Dominican, who wanted to provide a home for the Dominican nuns. The site chosen was the ninth-century Chiesetta di Santa Maria Magnanapoli. Work began in 1569 but was not completed until 1663.

During the course of nearly a century, as progress on the church continued, the design work fell to a series of well-known architects, beginning with Giacomo Della Porta and ending with Vincenzo Della Greca, who designed the ornate facade.

The main altar and one of the three chapels are the work of the great Baroque artist Gian Lorenzo Bernini. In 1932 the church became the chapel of the adjacent Pontifical College of St. Thomas Aquinas.

PLATE 45

PORTA SAN PAOLO

Today, this bucolic scene is a major traffic roundabout.

One of the eighteen gates in the Aurelian Wall, the Porta San Paolo leads out of the city center toward the port city of Ostia, the airport, and the beach. The wall was begun in AD 270 by Emperor Aurelius, who was desperate to find an effective way of intercepting invading barbarians. It was never meant to sustain a long attack, but to delay the sort of guerrilla warfare practiced by the "unwashed hordes" who regularly plundered unprotected areas of the city. Much of the wall's twelve and a half miles still remain, enclosing the legendary seven hills, the Campus Martius (the old martial training ground), and the Trastevere district.

In 1905 a person could stroll or take a carriage through the gate and find oneself in the countryside. Today the walls no longer encircle the entire city but only its historic center, now officially a municipal subdivision known as Municipio I. Rome's urban sprawl is defined as either "within the walls" or "outside the walls." For example, a standard taxi fare applies when coming from the airport to any destination "within the walls," and it is common to hear someone say that rents are lower "outside the walls."

The Porta San Paolo looks so much like a castle that it is sometimes called the *castellitto*. The Romans called it the Porta Ostienses, but its name was changed when the Basilica di San Paolo Fuori le Mura, Saint Paul's Basilica Outside the Walls, was built. In AD 386 a colonnade, a mile and a half in length and lined with eighty-one marble columns, was built to protect people from the elements as they walked from the gate to the basilica, but it has long since disappeared.

Roma - Piramide di Caio Cestio e Porta San Paolo

PLATE 46

THE COLOSSEUM IN A STORM

Reduced to a dark silhouette, the arena seems to remind us that
both man and beast died there in astonishing numbers.

Although the gladiatorial games had gone out of fashion long before, they were not officially abolished until the fifth century when, according to legend, St. Telemachus jumped into the arena to try and stop the violence, only to be stoned to death by an outraged crowd. The belief that Christians were martyred in the Colosseum did not emerge until the sixteenth century, when the arena began to be considered a sacred site. Pope Pius V admonished people to pick up sand from the grounds there, which he said was soaked with Christian blood. A hundred years later, Pope Benedict XIV established the stations of the cross around the Colosseum's interior ring, and a cross was erected in its center.

All that was over by 1905. With the secular government and the reunification of Italy, the Colosseum became a place of archaeological research and a national monument. In his *Pictures from Italy*, Charles Dickens wrote, "To see it crumbling there, an inch a year ... is to see the ghost of old Rome, wicked, wonderful city, haunting the very ground on which its people trod. It is the most impressive, the most stately, the most solemn, grand, majestic, mournful sight conceivable. Never, in its bloodiest prime, can the sight of the gigantic Coliseum, full and running over with the lustiest life, have moved one heart, as it must move all who look upon it now, a ruin. God be thanked: a ruin!"

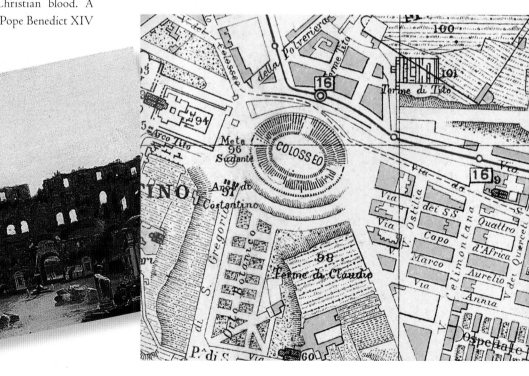

PLATE 47

ARCH OF TITUS FROM THE ARCH OF CONSTANTINE

Constantine was Rome's first Christian emperor.

The arch commemorates not only a battle but also a turning point in history. As he was about to enter a crucial battle against the forces of Emperor Maxentius, Constantine had a vision in which he saw in the sky the Greek letters "chi" and "rho," the first two letters of Christ's name, together with the words "By this sign, conquer." Constantine won the battle against an army much larger than his own, and took it as a sign that he should adopt Christianity. Rome's first Christian emperor thereby allowed the religion to flourish.

Pisa's image gives us a view of the elaborate decorations on the arch, which are a mix of carvings created in the time of Constantine and works stolen from other parts of the Forum. The roundel in the middle of the arch represents the Roman sun god. The use of a pagan image by a Christian emperor might seem puzzling, but historians speculate that Constantine needed to include some pagan imagery to pacify a still very strong and vocal non-Christian presence in the senate. The relief at the top was probably taken from the Forum of Trajan. It depicts a battle scene from the Dacian wars during the reign of either Domitian or Trajan. The statue atop the Corinthian column was also taken from the Forum of Trajan, and is one of eight, representing Dacian prisoners of war.

Today the arch is surrounded by a protective fence, and the bucolic scene Pisa depicted has been replaced with views of traffic from the Via dei Fori Imperiali, constructed during the Mussolini era, which now runs alongside the Forum.

PLATE 48

MEDIEVAL HOUSE AT TIVOLI

In the Middle Ages, the tiny hilltop town of Tivoli rivaled Rome itself.

During the era of the Roman Empire, Tibur, modern-day Tivoli, was a popular resort, its natural beauty enhanced by copious sulfur-rich springs. Of the many villas built here during this period, the most famous is the Villa Adrian, built by Emperor Hadrian. The emperors Augustus and Macenas also had villas in Tibur, as did the poet Horace.

From the tenth century onward, Tivoli was an independent city with its own elected consuls, rivaling Rome in a struggle for control over the region now known as Lazio. Because of the conflict with Rome, which endured for centuries, many of the houses also served as fortress towers. In 1461 Pope Pius II built the Rocca Pia as a symbol of the might of papal rule—this monumental castle still dominates the town.

At the height of the Renaissance, Roman noble families extended their efforts to the nearby resort of Tivoli. Many lavish villas were constructed during this period, most notably the glorious Villa d'Este.

In 1825 Pope Gregory XVI built his Villa Gregoriana in Tivoli, constructing it around a waterfall on the Aniene River. He created the fall by tunneling under the Monte Catillo, providing himself with an impressive garden and at the same time protecting Tivoli from flooding.

The walled city, just an hour's drive from Rome, is essentially just as it was half a millennium ago, and it is still possible to wander through narrow streets lined with medieval houses, many of which have been converted into trendy little shops, restaurants, and cafés.

A STREET AT TIVOLI.

PLATE 49

ILEX AVENUE AND FOUNTAIN (*FONTANA SCURA*), VILLA BORGHESE

Two fountains, shaded by trees, flank the monumental Borghese casino, now a museum.

In the seventeenth century, when Cardinal Scipione Borghese built his famous villa in order to house his enormous art collection, he commissioned two fountains to flank its entrance. They have become known as the *fontane scure*, the shaded fountains, as they were placed in a stand of trees.

The villa and its gardens remained in the Borghese family until 1901 when, after a long legal battle, the property was bought by the state and, following the wishes of King Umberto I, ceded to the city of Rome, becoming a public park and museums.

Mary Alsop King Waddington, an aristocratic American who often visited the gardens during her stay in Rome in 1879, was astonished to see it again on her return in 1904. "They have made extraordinary changes since the government has bought it," she wrote. "They have opened out new roads and paths, planted quantities of trees and flowers, and cleaned up and trimmed in every direction. It will be a splendid promenade in the heart of the city, but no longer the Villa Borghese we used to know, with ragged, unkempt corners, and little paths in out-of-way places, so choked up with weeds and long grass that one could hardly get through."

PLATE 50

"HOUSE OF COLA DI RIENZO," BY PONTE ROTTO

At the turn of the twentieth century, visitors were entranced by the ruins of this medieval house.

Nicolas Crescenzi, scion of an aristocratic Roman family, built this house in the eleventh century, as the inscription above the door plainly states. It was strategically placed along the river, near what is called the Ponte Rotto—"the broken bridge"—to protect the family interests, during a time when Rome was in a chaotic state, being ruled by a warring nobility. The building most probably served as a fortress tower as well as a home. Crescenzi used fragments of ancient Roman buildings as decoration, and imitated a classic Roman portico with columns.

For some time it was thought to have been the home of Cola di Rienzo, a legendary figure who led a people's uprising against the nobility in 1347, and attempted to unite Italy. His visions of grandeur were short-lived, however. During his six-month reign, he knighted himself, appointed himself king in a grand coronation ceremony, and invited all the nobles to a grand banquet, where he arrested them, only to abruptly pardon them all as they pleaded for their lives. The nobles, who did not find this at all humorous, vowed to take revenge, and Cola di Rienzo was lynched by a mob and fled to the Castel Sant'Angelo, where his faithful wife joined him, disguised as a young monk.

The house was also sometimes called the "Casa di Pilate," since it served as the setting for Pilate's palace during medieval miracle plays. After the Crescenzi family abandoned the house in the fourteenth century, it was used as a stable. In 1858 the pontifical government took over the property, and eventually gave it to the city of Rome. Although only the ground floor remained, it was restored and was used as the offices of the city's civil engineering department until 1960.

PLATE 51

SAN CLEMENTE, CHOIR AND TRIBUNE OF UPPER CHURCH

Like a layered cake, this twelfth-century church was built over a fourth-century church,
which in turn was built over a first-century house and temple.

In 1857 Father James Mulhooly, then prior of the Basilica di San Clemente, was unconvinced that the church was indeed the fourth-century relic it was presumed to be. An older building, he thought, must lie beneath it. So he began to dig. With generous financial support from Pope Pius IX, Mulhooly managed, within his lifetime, to uncover the fourth-century church beneath it. What the excavations ultimately revealed was that in 384 a church was built on top of what had been a Roman house and an adjacent Mithraic temple.

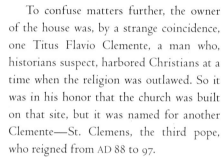

To confuse matters further, the owner of the house was, by a strange coincidence, one Titus Flavio Clemente, a man who, historians suspect, harbored Christians at a time when the religion was outlawed. So it was in his honor that the church was built on that site, but it was named for another Clemente—St. Clemens, the third pope, who reigned from AD 88 to 97.

A century later, in 1084, the church was looted and burned when the Normans sacked Rome. The Romans lost no time in building another church on top of it, completing the construction in 1108. As much as could be salvaged was placed in this new church, which is what confounded everyone into thinking it was much older than it was.

In 1667, when the English banished the Catholic Church in Ireland, San Clemente was given to the Irish Dominicans, who have presided over it ever since. Pisa's painting shows us the magnificent twelfth-century Byzantine mosaic, "The Cross as the Tree of Life," and the fourth-century white marble choir from the original church.

PLATE 52

SANTA MARIA IN COSMEDIN

At the turn of the twentieth century, tourists flocked to this newly restored medieval church.

In 1909 the traveler Olive Muriel Potter wrote, "This church is a gem of beauty, which Time and the Tiber and the vandals of the sixteenth and seventeenth centuries have been unable to rob of its glory." In fact, it also withstood both the earthquake of 860 and the Norman invasion of 1085.

It was one of the first medieval churches in Rome to be restored, reopening in 1899, freshly stripped of its Baroque facade. Originally built in 782 by Hadrian I on the site of a Greek temple to Hercules, it later became a refuge for Greeks fleeing persecution in Byzantium. Its name, Cosmedin, comes from the Greek word *kosmidion,* meaning "beautiful," which also gave us the English word "cosmetic." In Pisa's painting, we can see the intricate mosaic floor, dating from the twelfth century, and the altar and throne, which date from the thirteenth.

The church is as much a tourist attraction now as it was then, although most visitors do not venture inside. They stop at the portico to see the large mask known as the Bocca della Verità, "the mouth of truth." Legend has it that if you tell a lie with your hand in the mouth of the mask, it will be bitten off. In the 1953 film *Roman Holiday,* Gregory Peck takes Audrey Hepburn to see the mask, and frightens her by pretending that his hand has been amputated. Archaeologists believe that the mask may have been an ancient manhole cover.

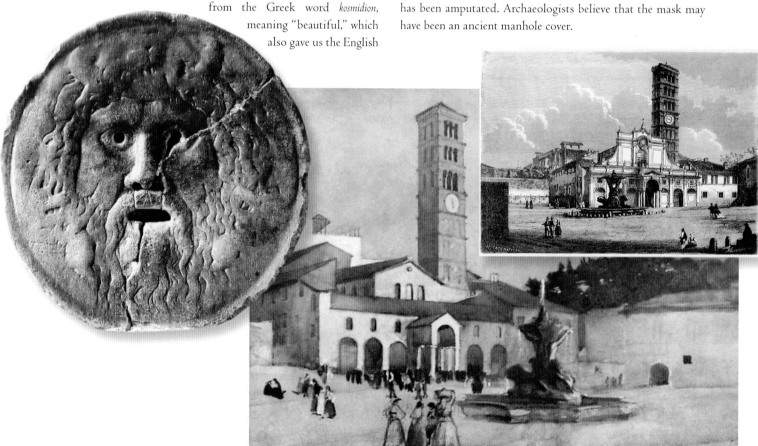

PLATE 53

CHAPEL OF SAN ZENO (*ORTO DEL PARADISO*) IN SAN PRASSEDE

This humble church is overlooked by today's visitors to Rome, but in 1905,
when medieval architecture was in fashion, it was a popular site.

Legend has it that in the first century, two sisters, Santa Prassede and Santa Pudenzia, both devout Catholics, made it a practice to gather the remains of Christian martyrs and collect their blood with sponges. They squeezed the blood into a well in their home, where it was kept with all reverence. Soon enough, the sisters were martyred themselves for the practice—not for their ghoulishness, but for their religious beliefs.

In 817 Pope Paschal I built a church over the site of the family home where the sisters had sheltered the early Christians. A slab in the floor marks the spot where the well once stood. Within this church, the pope built a beautiful little chapel to San Zeno, which would be the final resting place of his mother, Theodora. Covered in glittering mosaics, it earns its medieval name, "Garden of Paradise."

Travelers in 1905 would have visited San Prassede to see one of the few remnants of medieval architecture still unspoiled by Baroque adornment, and the Chapel of San Zeno, which contains the most important example of Byzantine mosaic work in Rome. Next to the chapel, a fragment of green jasper is displayed in a niche, protected by a grate. It was brought back from the Crusades by Cardinal Giovanni Colonna, and is said to be part of the column to which Christ was bound when he was flayed.

PLATE 54

CLOISTERS OF ST. PAUL'S-WITHOUT-THE-WALLS

The medieval cloister is all that remains of the original church, which was rebuilt after a massive fire.

Given the early twentieth-century passion for medieval architecture, it is no surprise that, of all the glories of the massive basilica, Alberto Pisa chose only to paint the cloisters. Emperor Constantine I originally began the church in 324, built over the grave of St. Paul, who is said to have been beheaded nearby on the Ostian Way.

As it was outside Rome's protective walls, it was vulnerable to invasion, and was sacked three times. The Lombards raided its treasures in 739, followed by the Saracens in 847. Pope John VIII, fearing further incursion, built a massive protective wall, completed in 882, enclosing not only the church but also an entire monastic village, which was inhabited until it was felled by an earthquake in 1348.

The pope's walls were not enough to prevent the forces of the French king Charles V from sacking St. Paul's once more in 1527. Each time the church was damaged, it was rebuilt in ever more grandiose fashion, so that by the seventeenth century it was one of the greatest churches in Rome, rivaled only by St. Peter's.

The story does not end here. In 1823 a massive fire destroyed St. Paul's. It was rebuilt with due attention to re-creating the antique architecture, and reconsecrated in 1840, but it was never quite the same. Miraculously, the early thirteenth-century Benedictine cloister, perhaps the most beautiful in Rome, remained untouched. Its graceful arches are supported by columns, each one different from the others—corkscrewed, serpentine, slender, or wide, encrusted with intricate mosaics of colorful marble fragments.

PLATE 55

CLOISTERS IN
SANTA SCHOLASTICA, SUBIACO

The monastery complex includes three cloisters, built in different styles.

Santa Scholastica, the oldest Benedictine monastery in the world, has been continuously inhabited by the order since the seventh century. A complex of buildings nestled in the mountains above the town of Subiaco, it has been damaged and rebuilt repeatedly over the centuries, resulting in a peculiar mixture of styles.

Of the monastery's three cloisters, Pisa has chosen to paint the one known as the Cosmatesque. The Cosmateci were a Roman family who were masters of the art of mosaic. During the twelfth and thirteenth centuries they created intricate marble floors in the great churches of Rome, as well as those in the Benedictine monasteries of Subiaco. Here the work is extremely restrained, using mostly natural shades of beige and gray marble in place of the exuberant color for

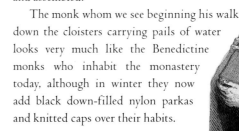

which they were better known. The arches in the Gothic style were probably built in pieces in Rome, then carried up the mountainside and assembled.

The monk whom we see beginning his walk down the cloisters carrying pails of water looks very much like the Benedictine monks who inhabit the monastery today, although in winter they now add black down-filled nylon parkas and knitted caps over their habits.

E. DUVERGER

PLATE 56

SANTA MARIA SOPRA MINERVA

Rome's only Gothic church was built over the Roman temples of Minerva, Isis, and Serapis.

In the early years of the twentieth century, the glories of the Renaissance—not to mention the excesses of the Baroque—were out of fashion. Of far greater value were the architectural remains of the Middle Ages, and the purity of ancient Roman ruins. The Basilica of Saint Mary over Minerva, near the Pantheon, was held in great esteem, as it is the only Gothic church in Rome, begun in 1280 by the Dominican friars Sisto and Ristoro, who also worked on Santa Maria Novella in Florence. Its most striking feature is the vaulted ceiling, decorated with stars, painted in gold leaf against a rich blue background, which was added in the nineteenth century but honors the Gothic style.

At the turn of the twentieth century, the church was the venue of choice for aristocratic weddings and funerals. The great actress Adelaide Ristori, whose career took her to the stages of Europe and the United States, married the marchesa Giuliano Capranica del Grillo here in 1847. When she died in 1906, her funeral mass was also held here.

Michelangelo's 1521 sculpture "Christ Bearing the Cross" and Filippino Lippi's frescoes, painted between 1488 and 1492, are the greatest of the church's many artistic treasures, along with monuments and busts by Gian Lorenzo Bernini. The body of Saint Catherine of Siena is buried here, though her head is kept in Siena. The room where she died in 1380, including its frescoes, was transported from nearby Via Santa Chiara and reconstructed within the church in 1630.

In the seventeenth century, the Dominicans discovered an Egyptian obelisk from the sixth century BC buried nearby, and erected it in the piazza, just outside the church doors. It is planted on the back of a marble elephant designed by Bernini. The Romans, in their dialect, called it Er Pulcino della Minerva—"Minerva's little chick."

PLATE 57

ST. PETER'S

Mark Twain, who visited St. Peter's frequently during his stay in Rome,
called it the "monster church," and declared himself unimpressed.

At the turn of the twentieth century, when travel took a long time and few could afford it, the Vatican was a lot less crowded than it is today. It seems incredible now, when the lines to get into the museum wind around the walls and it takes an hour or more to get inside, that a trip to the Vatican was then a casual, spur-of-the-moment thing. Visitors to Rome stayed for weeks or months, and made Vatican visits whenever they found themselves with a little time to kill.

In a letter written in 1904, Mary Worthington reported, "It was coming down in buckets when we came out of the concert and a drive seemed insane, so I suggested a turn in St. Peter's (which is always a good resource on a rainy day)."

In the spring of 1900 Oscar Wilde wrote to Robert Ross, "Today, on coming out of the Vatican Gallery, Greek gods and Roman middle-classes in my brain, all marble to make the contrast worse, I found that the Vatican Gardens were open to the Bohemian and the Portuguese pilgrims. I at once spoke both languages fluently, explained that my English dress was a form of penance, and entered that waste, desolate park, with its faded Louis XIV gardens, its sombre avenues, its sad woodland. The peacocks screamed, and I understood why tragedy dogged the gilt feet of each pontiff."

Alberto Pisa has chosen to paint just a corner of the great facade, focusing on Maderno's granite fountain, which is one of a pair flanking the great obelisk. The other was designed by Bernini.

PLATE 58

INTERIOR OF ST. PETER'S, THE BRONZE STATUE OF ST. PETER

Centuries of fervent kisses have nearly worn away the big toe of this thirteenth-century bronze statue.

It is a telling sign of just how much the works of the Renaissance and the Baroque were disdained in the early twentieth century, that Pisa's assignment bypassed the great splendors of Bernini, Borromini—even Michelangelo's "Pietà"—in favor of this medieval statue.

Today, historians agree that it is almost surely the work of Arnolfo di Cambio, a leading sculptor of tombs and decorator of churches, who also worked on the interiors of Santa Maria Maggiore and Santa Maria in Aracoeli. In a letter dated Palm Sunday, March 28, 1904, Mary Alsop King Waddington, the American widow of a French diplomat, wrote, "We stopped some time at the great bronze statue of Saint Peter. I was astounded at the quantity and quality of people who came up and kissed the toe of the Saint. Priests and nuns, of course, and old people, both men and women, but it seemed extraordinary to me to see young men, tall, good-looking fellows, bend down quite as reverently as the others and kiss the toe."

According to the New Testament, St. Peter's feet were washed by Christ; thus the holy foot, and particularly its most accessible toe, has always been the most revered part of the statue's anatomy.

PLATE 59

A CARDINAL IN VILLA D'ESTE

In 1905 the villa was still the private residence of the princes of the Church.

Cardinal Ippolito d'Este, who built this spectacular villa in the sixteenth century, stipulated in his will that it should be passed down to succeeding cardinals. He would have been heartbroken to learn that by the middle of the nineteenth century his masterpiece had fallen into decay, neglected by his heirs.

It was sold to the House of Hapsburg, who did nothing to preserve it. Then along came Cardinal Gustav von Hohenlohe, a German prince who had been fascinated by the place since his childhood. He persuaded the Hapsburgs to cede to him the rights to the villa on the condition that he would restore the great house and its once-magnificent terraced water gardens. Until his death in 1893, the villa was Cardinal Hohenlohe's home. He returned it to its former glory, and made it a cultural center, hosting not only members of the church hierarchy but also famous musicians, artists, and heads of state.

In 1918, at the end of World War I, the villa became the property of the Italian state. Between the two World Wars, the villa was open to the public, but the Allied bombing of 1944 caused much damage, and it has been under reconstruction almost continuously since the 1950s. Today the villa and its gardens are visited by thousands of people every day, but in the evening, when quiet falls once again, it is possible to imagine how it must have been in 1905 when a cardinal and his aide could enjoy a solitary walk among the fountains.

PLATE 60

VILLA D'ESTE—PATH OF THE HUNDRED FOUNTAINS

The water gardens at the Villa d'Este are among the most extensive in the world.

Pisa's painting gives us only a glimpse of the wondrous fountains, paths, and waterfalls in the villa's glorious terraced gardens. The path of a hundred fountains, which steps down through several levels of a steep incline, is lined with fountains of every kind.

The water garden was originally conceived and built by Cardinal Ippolito d'Este in 1560, and was expanded by his successor, Cardinal Alessandro d'Este. Alessandro d'Este spent ten years, from 1605 to 1615, adding the latest technological wonders, including an immense waterfall designed by Gian Lorenzo Bernini.

By the eighteenth century the gardens had fallen into a state of disrepair, and the property passed into the hands of the German House of Hapsburg. Cardinal Gustav von Hohenlohe acquired the property in 1851 and began an extensive restoration of the water gardens.

The composer Franz Liszt was a frequent guest at the villa. He was enchanted by the musical sound of the rippling fountains and cascading falls, which inspired him to compose many works there, including the piano piece, "Les Jeux d'Eau à la Villa d'Este."

PLATE 61

THEATRE OF MARCELLUS

In the Middle Ages, this classic theater was converted into a fortress against the invading barbarians.

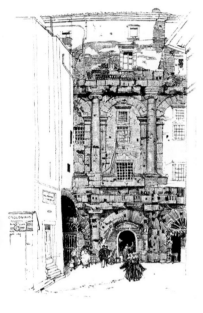

A century before the Colosseum was built, Julius Caesar planned a sumptuous theater to compete with a similar one built by his predecessor, Pompey. Alas, poor Caesar was assassinated before construction began. In 13 BC, Augustus finished it as a gift to his beloved nephew Marcellus, the son of his sister Ottavia. Marcellus in turn died at the age of twenty-five, five years before the theater opened its doors. Seating 15,000 spectators, it was the scene of classic tragedies and comedies. As the building is just a few feet from the Tiber, it was vulnerable to sacking, and the once-magnificent travertine marble was blackened during the Middle Ages, then stolen during the Renaissance for various projects of the Catholic Church. By the sixteenth century, the wealthy and noble Orsini family had appropriated the real estate and built a palace for themselves on the top level.

When Pisa made this painting, small shops occupied the lower levels, and the former Orsini Palace had been divided into a series of luxurious apartments. Olave Potter, writing in 1909, lamented, "Its blackened stones have a somber, tragic aspect. They frown down upon the cheerful piazza below, where *contadini* with their brightly painted carts lounge through the sunny day."

Many visitors arriving in Rome today mistake the theater for its much larger relative, the Colosseum. The shops are gone, but the luxurious apartments remain, and in the summer the courtyard is used for concerts.

PLATE 62

ISLAND OF THE TIBER—
THE ISOLA SACRA

The Tiber's only island has been the site of a hospital for more than 2,000 years.

The Tiber Island, the Isola Tiberina, has variously been known as Isola di San Bartolomeo, the Isola Sacra, and for reasons made obvious by Pisa's painting, the Island Between Two Bridges. According to legend, in 510 BC, when the Romans drove the tyrant King Tarquinius out of town, they threw all his grain reserves into the river, forming the basis for the island. In about 293 BC, Rome suffered from a terrible plague. Consulting the book of the oracle Sybil, the city rulers determined to send a delegation to the temple of the god of medicine, Aesclepius, in Epidaurus. While the delegates were there, a snake slithered out from under the statue of the Greek god and onto their boat. As they sailed up the Tiber on their return to Rome, the snake left the boat and clambered onto the island, which they took as a sign. A hospital was built there, along with a temple to Aesclepius and smaller temples to seven other gods, which is why it became known as the Isola Sacra, or "sacred island." To further commemorate the event, the island itself was modeled with walls in the form of a ship.

Since an island made an ideal quarantine area, it continued to be used as a hospital for centuries. In 1584 the order of San Giovanni di Dio built a hospital there, which today is a busy modern facility. It is known as the Ospidale Fattebenefratelli, because—so they say—the brothers once put a sign on their alms box reading "Fatte bene fratelli!" (Do good, brothers!)

The island is also the site of a beautiful church, built over the ruins of Aesclepius' temple in AD 998 and eventually dedicated to Saint Bartholomew. In the painting we see the bell tower rising above the other buildings. Today, the island is known as the Isola Tiberina, but in 1905, before the Fascists set about renaming places, the island was often called the Isola di San Bartolomeo.

The two connecting bridges, which gave the island its fourth name, date to Roman times. The Ponte Fabricio, on the right in the painting, is the oldest bridge in Rome. First built in 62 BC, it is still almost intact today, connecting the island to the old ghetto district. The Ponte Cestio, seen on the left, connects the island to Trastevere. It was constructed in 46 BC and has been largely rebuilt, although remnants of the original bridge were retained.

PLATE 63

THE STEPS OF ARA COELI

Now, as in 1905, this famous staircase provides exercise for the energetic tourist
prepared to scale the 124 steps.

The main entrance to the Church of Santa Maria in Ara Coeli is approached by a truly daunting staircase, a steep 124 steps leading from the street below to the very top of the Capitoline, the highest of Rome's seven hills. A grateful Rome built the staircase in 1348, a tribute for having been largely spared the horrors of

the "black plague." At that time, the papacy had moved to Avignone, and Rome was in a state of decay. There was little money for such a grandiose project, so it was decided that the marble for the staircase should be taken from the Colosseum. Sadly, the idea caught on, and the Colosseum as well as other Roman ruins were repeatedly scavenged in the ensuing years. In the Middle Ages, the staircase provided stadium seating for spectators who came to watch the executions of convicted criminals at the foot of the steps.

Centuries later, during the 1930s, an ancient Roman "insula," a multistoried apartment house with three stores on the ground level, was unearthed at the former site of these executions. Today, the steep steps are amazingly crowded with energetic tourists willing to make the long climb. In 1905 visitors might have been more likely to ascend the gentler slope from the Forum and enter through a side door.

PLATE 64

STEPS OF THE CHURCH OF SAINTS DOMENICO AND SISTO

The Baroque steps topped by a cloudy sky provide a typical view of a corner of Rome.

These sixteenth-century steps are a fine example of the Italian Baroque. Positioned at the top of a hill, near the ancient Trajan's Market, they back onto the Quirinal, now the seat of the Italian government. The steps originally led to a monastery complex with an adjoining church, built in 1569 under the auspices of Pope Pius V. Having been a Dominican himself, he wanted to leave a lasting legacy to the order—and he did it in grand style.

Richly decorated in marbles and frescoes, the church boasts a high altar and a chapel by the great Gian Lorenzo Bernini, and the porticos of the monastery cloister are attributed to Jacopo Barozzi da Vignola, appointed chief architect of Saint Peter's after the death of Michelangelo.

Sadly for the public, the Baroque splendors of the monastery and church are no longer easily accessible. In 1931 the International College of Dominicans, often known as the Angelicum, were evicted from their ancestral home at the convent of Santa Maria Sopra Minerva near the Pantheon. They needed a new building, so they negotiated with the monks of Domenico and Sisto to take over the monastery and turn it into a Dominican college.

The college was originally founded in 1577 to train clergy for missionary work in the New World, with both Spanish and Italian instructors. In 1963 it became the Pontifical University of Saint Thomas Aquinas, and today is known particularly for its faculties of ecclesiastical law and Thomistic philosophy.

PLATE 65

SANTA MARIA MAGGIORE

The imposing church on the Esquiline Hill was on the itinerary of turn-of-the-century travelers,
who admired the medieval architecture, while lamenting the Baroque additions.

The monumental Santa Maria Maggiore, built by Pope Liberius around AD 360, earns the title *maggiore* by virtue of its size. It is the largest church devoted to the Virgin Mary, and the only church in Rome whose core remained intact after the earthquake of 1348. Its bell tower, constructed in the fourteenth century, is the tallest in Rome. In the eighteenth century its medieval exterior was encased in a Baroque facade, but the classical style of the basilica's interior was left untouched.

It is a mecca for religious pilgrims as well as a magnet for lovers of art, who come to see the frescoes by Guido Reni, the sculptures by Arnolfo di Cambio and Bernini, and the magnificent Sangallo ceiling. In *Italian Hours*, Henry James wrote, "The deeper charm is in the social or historic note or tone or atmosphere of the church—I fumble, you see, for the right expression; the sense it gives you, in common with most of the

Roman churches, and more than any of them, of having been prayed in for several centuries by an endlessly curious and complex society."

The view Pisa paints downplays the imposing size and magnificence of the church itself in favor of portraying the large piazza it faces, whose apparent tranquility has been ruined in the intervening century by a profusion of cars, buses, and taxis. The column in the piazza, topped by a statue of the Virgin Mary, acknowledges her help in saving Rome from the plague.

"Big Mary" (as the church is affectionately known to Rome's English-speaking residents) is the province of the pope himself, who presides over the Feast of the Assumption from a special papal altar each year on August 15. Otherwise, church duties are delegated to an archpriest—an archbishop appointed as a cardinal.

PLATE 66

ARCH OF CONSTANTINE

The arch is one of the most recent constructions in the Forum.

Constantine's Arch, completed in 315, is by Roman Forum standards almost modern. It celebrates Constantine's triumph over his co-emperor, Maxentius. Since Constantine is remembered as one of Rome's "good" emperors and Maxentius as one of the "bad" ones, there was reason to rejoice. Constantine was the first Roman emperor to embrace the Catholic faith and stop the persecution of Christians, but he also moved the capital of the empire to what is now Istanbul, a city that he called Constantinople. This was a bad omen for Rome, which soon began to decline and decay.

The arch was the highlight of triumphal marches. As emperors entered the city covered in glory, they marched along the Via Triumphalis, which began in the Campus Martius, circled the Circus Maximus, rounded the Palatine Hill, then went right through Constantine's Arch, winding up on the Capitoline.

The arch's decorations are something of a jumble, combining new work with friezes lifted from other monuments created centuries earlier. Some historians believe that one can experience an entire sweep of Roman decorative work just by studying this one arch. It has been suggested that all the borrowing was a desperate attempt to finish the arch within a relatively short time period—it was built in just three years. Restoration of the arch began in the eighteenth century, and continued up to the late 1990s, when the Forum was spruced up for the new millennium celebrations.

PLATE 67

CASTEL AND PONTE SANT'ANGELO

The last act of Puccini's *Tosca*, which premiered in 1904, takes place atop this fortress.

The clock is gone and the dress of the passers-by has changed, but this view of the castle and bridge is remarkably unchanged since Pisa painted it. The castle has seen many reincarnations in its long life. It was first built in 139 by Emperor Hadrian as a tomb for himself and his family. He died the year before it was completed, and his ashes were interred in a sepulchre within the structure. The round shape of the building echoes that of the Etruscan tombs, but it is much larger, befitting the emperor of the Roman Empire. The top of the building was covered with earth and planted with cypress trees, surrounded by alternating columns and statues.

In 271, as repeated sackings of Rome began, the castle was incorporated into the protective wall built by the emperor, and remained a strategic part of Rome's defenses for the next thousand years. In 537, when Rome was attacked by the Goths, soldiers atop the castle drove them off by hurling Hadrian's statues and columns down at them.

During the plague years of the sixth century, Pope Gregory the Great ordered a march through the city. Thousands followed him, praying for mercy as they went, many of them falling dead along the way. Just as the pope reached the castle, he is said to have seen a vision of an angel sheathing its sword, a sign that the plague was over. From that time, an angel has topped the castle, replacing the original statue of Hadrian.

In the nineteenth century, the lower levels of the castle were used as a prison for high-ranking criminals, including Beatrice Cenci, Benvenuto Cellini, and many of those arrested during the citizens' uprising against the French occupation, including Puccini's hero, the fictional painter Cavaradossi. Today it is a museum, and the scene of a lively summer festival. The panorama from the top terrace, which is open to the public, is one of the most breathtaking in Rome.

PLATE 68

BRONZE STATUE OF
MARCUS AURELIUS ON THE CAPITOL

In 1905 this ancient statue was considered the main attraction of the Capitoline Square.

The work of Michelangelo and, indeed, all of "modern" architecture—now known as the Renaissance and the Baroque—were not held in high regard at the turn of the twentieth century. The trapezoid square he designed for the Capitoline, now considered a work of sublime genius, was, in the words of Henry James, "an unfailing disappointment." In *A Roman Holiday*, James wrote, "The hill is so low, the ascent so narrow, Michael Angelo's architecture in the quadrangle at the top so meagre, the whole place so much more of a mole-hill than a mountain, that for the first ten minutes of your standing there, Roman history seems to have sunk through a trap door." Mark Twain, in *The Innocents Abroad*, likewise expressed his weariness of the great Renaissance architect: "I have never felt so fervently thankful, so soothed, so tranquil, so filled with a blessed peace as I did yesterday when I learned that Michelangelo was dead."

The statue of Marcus Aurelius is the only one of its kind to have survived from antiquity, and is considered the model for all

subsequent equestrian monuments. It would have been destroyed with all the other pagan statues, had the church not mistaken Marcus Aurelius for Constantine, the first Christian emperor. Pope Paul III had it moved from its original place at St. Giovanni in Laterano, against the objections of Michelangelo, who thought that it should stay where the ancient Romans put it. In 1990 the original statue was brought inside the Capitoline Museum and restored. What we see in the piazza today is an exact replica.

PLATE 69

ST. PETER'S FROM THE PINCIAN GARDENS

In 1905 the Pincian Hill was the scene of afternoon strolls and socializing.

The narrow road that runs from the church of the Trinità dei Monti at the top of the Spanish Steps, past the Villa Medici and the Pincian Gardens to the Piazza del Popolo, was a favorite late-afternoon outing. There were very few cars in Rome at that time, and when they appeared, with some wealthy aristocrat or other behind the wheel, they always attracted a crowd; but there were plenty of open horse-drawn carriages, and walking was still a noble pastime. It was the habit of Pope Pius IX to take an afternoon ride over the Pincio in his papal carriage, which was drawn by a team of white mules. Fashionable Rome followed his example, and the Pincian Hill became a place to see and be seen, whether in a carriage or on foot. In either case, the views of Rome from the hill were—and still are—magnificent, especially at twilight.

Émile Zola described the scene better than anyone in his novel *Rome*: "Then Dario ordered the coachman to drive up to the Pincio, for the round of the Pincio is obligatory on fine, clear afternoons. And from the beautiful terrace, so broad and lofty, one of the most beautiful views of Rome was offered to the gaze. Beyond the Tiber, beyond the pale chaos of the new district of the castle meadows, and between the greenery of Monte Mario and the Janiculum, arose St. Peter's."

PLATE 70

FROM THE TERRACE OF
THE HOUSE OF DOMITIAN

Emperor Domitian's palace had the most impressive view on the Palatine Hill.

During the era of the Roman Empire, the Palatine Hill was the location of choice for Rome's mightiest families. Domitian, who built the most impressive palace of all for his Flavian family, naturally had the best view, which allowed him to look directly down into the Circus Maximus.

By 1905 medieval and Renaissance buildings had changed the landscape, but the view was no less impressive. Now, as then, the terrace of Domitian's palace provides a vista of Rome's confluence of the ancient and the merely very old. To the right we see the bell tower of the Chiesa di Santa Francesca

Romana, built in the Forum over the former Temple of Venus, and dedicated in 1425. To the left are the ruins of the great Basilica di Maxentius, which was completed by Constantine, the first Christian emperor of Rome, in AD 312. Nearby is the Arch of Titus, erected to commemorate the fall of Jerusalem in AD 70.

ROMA.

PALATINO E CIRCO MASSIMO.

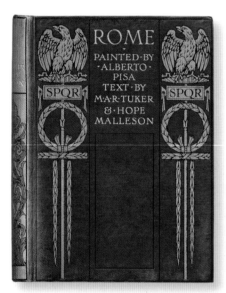

Rome was the first European city to be illustrated in A&C Black's 20 Shilling Series of color plate books. It was published on April 4, 1905, in the usual edition of 3,000 copies, together with a large paper edition of 250, signed "A&C Black," to sell at two guineas. The cyanine blue cloth of the trade edition, particularly the spine, which is often exposed to light, is prone to fading. The cover design is by A. A. Turbayne's Carlton Studios, whose monogram can be seen at the lower right on the spine.

The publication of the A&C Black volume came a few months behind that of *Rome and Its Story* by Lina Duff Gordon and St. Clair Baddeley, with illustrations by Aubrey Waterfield, which was published by the rival British publisher Dent. In October 1904, Adam Black wrote to Miss Tuker, the author of their *Rome*, to say, "Dent have to some extent 'scored' by appearing first but if their 'Rome' is like their recently published 'Paris', we shall eventually win easily." A number of other publishers were trying to emulate A&C Black's success with this sort of color plate book, but none succeeded.

Rome was reprinted in 1911 and 1915, though copies do not necessarily indicate whether they are reprints or not. A safer guide is that early copies have the top edges in gilt, and that, as the eagle-eyed Miss Tuker

The trade edition of *Rome* with its royal blue cover (left); *Rome and Its Story*, published by Dent in 1904 (below left); and the large paper edition of A&C Black's *Rome*, signed "A&C Black" in hand on the front free endpaper (below).

pointed out at the time of publication, the captions to the illustrations on pages 154 and 224 are wrongly transposed. Advertisements for other books, bound in at the back, can also be used as a guide.

The authors, Hope Malleson and Mildred Anna Rosalie Tuker, were two friends, then in their forties. They had written the *Handbook to Christian and Ecclesiastical Rome* for A&C Black, published in several volumes a few years earlier, so could be expected to know their subject well. Malleson and Tuker were first contacted in November 1903, and offered £100 for 60,000–70,000 words, eventually writing 67,500. Several chapters had appeared previously in *Monthly Review*, *Broad Views*, *Macmillan's Magazine*, and the *Hibbert Journal*.

Alberto Pisa was offered £2 each for the right to reproduce seventy illustrations, somewhat below what A&C Black usually offered.

A review in the *Studio* welcomed the book as "Decidedly one of the most best of the many coloured books recently issued by Messrs. Black, the 'Rome' cannot fail to delight all lovers of the City of the Seven Hills, so well do the numerous illustrations interpret her most characteristic features with the effects of sunlight which add so greatly to their charm, and so thoroughly in touch with the spirit of their theme are the authors who have collaborated in the text." *Rome* was later published in the "Popular and New Series" of the 1920s, with just thirty-two illustrations. Rafael Tuck issued two series of postcards reproduced from the *Rome* illustrations.

Miss Tuker's other work includes *The Past and Future of Ethics* (OUP, 1938), in which she proposed that "man" connote the human race, and "wer" or "werman" be the male person. She spelled the gender "femel" to avoid the suggestion that it is subsidiary to the male. She was an ardent campaigner for women's rights, and in 1954 her executors gave the Women's Library in east London "a large consignment of material on the position of women."

The two-sided color advertisement for *Rome* produced by A&C Black to be placed by booksellers in copies of other books in the series.

A New World of Color Printing

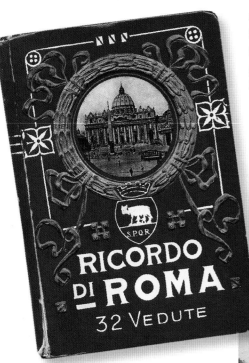

The cultured classes of the first decade of the twentieth century loved color, and great strides in printing and ink technology allowed them to have it, breaking free of the limitations of the monotone pages of their parents' generation with their woodcuts and steel engravings. Many of these developments came from Germany where, by the turn of the nineteenth century, there was a lucrative industry in color postcards, greeting cards, and books containing dozens of color illustrations.

The challenge and promise of color were quickly taken up in Britain, where presses—especially in London and Edinburgh—started to use the latest technology to print color plates for a range of reference books.

Until the early 1890s, anyone wanting to print a color image had to design the images in such a way that the different colors, each printed from its own plate, could easily be separated from each other. Many ways were developed to create subtlety in the use of color, including engraving fine detail into each color plate, using separate plates for different tones of the same color, and finishing each plate by hand after it had been printed. Even so, most color printing in 1900 was fairly crude, and it is clear—especially under the magnifying glass—that the drive for realistic color still had some way to go.

The best color printing in the 1900s, however, was stunning. In the period between 1900 and 1914, before war dried up ink and machinery supplies from Germany to the rest of the world, printing in color reached a peak that was not to be reached again until the 1960s.

It is important to remember that outdoor color photography as we know it, using color film to photograph places and people, was not invented until

Ricordo di Roma is a typical 1900s tourist souvenir containing a concertina-fold sheet of thirty-two views, or *vedute*, with a caption on the back of each image in Italian, French, English, and German (above). The colored photograph of the Tempio de Venere is from *Ricordo di Roma Parte II* of about 1905 (right).

the 1930s. However, from about 1890 onward, several processes for making color photographs of inanimate objects in a studio setting were well advanced, and the printers of the period were amazingly inventive.

One of the greatest pioneers was a German emigrant, Carl Hentschel, who in the 1890s patented the Hentschel Colourtype Process and set up his company on London's Fleet Street. Hentschel developed a massive camera that used three color filters—red, green, and blue—to capture simultaneous images of any original flat color image. At the same time, developments such as the halftone screen, which allowed color gradation to be printed as an almost-imperceptible pattern of different-sized dots onto paper, were enabling photographed images to be transferred to paper, both in black and white and in the new three-color process.

It was now possible to photograph flat objects like paintings—or small groups of objects in a studio setting—in color. And it was possible to use those images, separated into their three component process colors, to print color images. It was impossible, however, to make color photographs of the wide outside world, of cities, mountains, and crowds of people. Yet once they had a taste of color postcards and color pictures in books, those who could afford to buy such relatively expensive luxuries wanted as much color as they could get.

The images in this book demonstrate the many ways in which the inventors, photographers, and publishers of the period strove to give their customers what they so craved—the real world on the printed page in full color.

The painitng of a Roman wine cart by Aubrey Waterfield is from *Rome and Its Story*, published by Dent in 1904 (below left). The two watercolors are from a ribbon-tied book of thirty-two paintings entitled *Roma*, published in about 1906 by A Graldi, Milan. The artist is not identified.

THE HENTSCHEL THREE-COLOR PROCESS

In 1868, when he was four years old, Carl Hentschel moved to London from the Russian-Polish city of Lodz with his family. Like his father, he became an engraver, and by 1900 was an important figure in color printing and in London's social life. As well as being an active advocate of his innovative printing process, he was a founding member of several clubs, including the Playgoer's Club and, as a great friend of Jerome K. Jerome, was the model for Harris in Jerome's *Three Men in a Boat.*

Although not the inventor of the three-color halftone process—it had been developed by Frenchmen Louis du Hauron and Charles Cros, and American Frederick Ives in the 1870s— Hentschel's company led the way in using the method on a commercial scale.

The process is well described in Burch's 1906 book *Colour Printing and Colour Printers.* "Once the principle is accepted that any combination of colours can be resolved into its primary elements, it remains only for the photographer to obtain three negatives which automatically dissect the original, making three distinct photographic records of the reds, yellows and blues which enter into the composition. The result is obtained by the use of transparent screens of coloured pigment or liquid, 'light filters' as they are technically termed, placed in front of the lens. These filters admit any two of the primary colours and absorb the other one. Three separate screens are employed, each with the

Carl Hentschel (top) and the original "three men in a boat" (below)—Carl Hentschel, George Wingrave, and Jerome K. Jerome.

The chromographoscope (right), invented by Louis Ducos du Hauron in 1874, was a dual-purpose machine. It could be used as a camera or as an additive viewer.

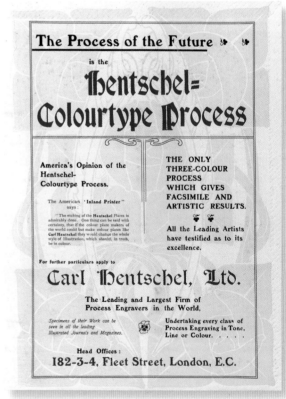

lines ruled at a different angle, and when the negative records of the colour analysis are obtained, the three photographs are converted into printing surfaces."

Among Hentschel's growing list of customers was Adam Black, the original "A" of A&C Black, who early on recognized the Colourtype process as the one that would give his publishing company a head start in the production of color books. In its time, it must have seemed magical that color plates could be produced to such a high standard and—at only four hours from photograph to finished printing plate—so quickly.

COLOR POSTCARDS

The first decade of the twentieth century was the high tide of the postcard craze, which used the new technologies of color printing and the newly introduced postcard postage rate to fill drawing rooms with pictures from all over the world. In 1899 the British Post Office gave in to popular pressure to allow postcards to have more than just the address written on the back, which allowed publishers to use all of the picture side to display their design. Other countries quickly followed suit.

The painting portraying a summer drink shop is by Aubrey Waterfield, from *Rome and Its Story*, published by Dent in 1904 (below left). The postcard of the Vatican Gardens with the dome of St. Peter's in the background dates from 1905, as does the postcard of the Grand Hotel du Quirinal with the Pantheon in the background.

196 ROMA - Giardino Vaticano - Con la cupola di S. Pietro.

GRAND HÔTEL DU QUIRINAL
ROME
PANTHEON

HOTEL FLORA - ROME

Position incomparable en face du Parc
de la Villa Borghese et du Pincio.

Unrivalled situation, rooms overlooking
the Borghese and Pincians's Gardens.

Aussicht auf die Parkanlagen der
Villa Borghese und des Pincio

Postcard publishers rapidly increased production to fill the demand for postcards, these cards being the one product line that constantly pushed color printing to the limits of what was achievable. Many color postcards were printed in Germany, or by companies with German origins. None was more inventive, productive, and formative than the London-based company of Raphael Tuck and Sons. Raphael Tuch (his original name) moved to London with his wife and eleven children from Breslau in Prussia in 1865. He opened a small shop in

Whitechapel, moving in 1870 to City Road, where he and his sons Adolph, Herman, and Gustave helped develop a range of photographs and scraps, much of it imported from Germany. In 1871 came the first Christmas card, and in 1876 the colored oleograph. The breakthrough year for the postcard was 1894, when Tuck produced a card with a vignette of Snowdon in North Wales.

In the first decades of the postcard's life, there were three ways of producing a color image. You either started with a real black-and-white photograph and added subtle layers of color to indicate water or a sunset, used traditional color engravers to create separated color designs from scratch, or used the new three-color process to photograph painted originals. It was this third option that allowed companies like Raphael Tuck and Sons to expand so rapidly, and they were quick to commission a number of excellent artists to create series of paintings specifically for reproduction as postcards.

The postcard advertising the Hotel Flora (opposite page, top) dates from the early 1920s and shows how typographic design standards had declined from the prewar years. The Arch of Titus (opposite, left) is a 1900 photochrome. The statue of Moses (opposite, right) is from the tourist souvenir *Ricordo di Roma Parte II.*

The Door of the Temple of Romulus, painted by Aubrey Waterfield, from *Rome and Its Story.*

PHOTOCHROMES

Of all the methods for colorizing photographic images before outdoor color photography, the photochrome process was probably the most successful. The brilliantly colored prints displayed at the 1889 Paris Exposition by the Swiss company Orell Füssli and Co. won a gold medal, and their realism thrilled those who saw them. Only three companies—Füssli's own Photoglob in Switzerland, Photochrom in Britain, and the Detroit Printing Company in the United States— were ever licensed to use the "secret" technique, which by 1910 had resulted in more than 13,000 color images of every corner of Europe and the landmarks of North America, India, and North Africa.

Each photochrome required intensive labor, an artistic eye, and, ideally, an accurate record of what colors were actually present in the scene portrayed. A film negative was used as the basis for creating a series of lithographic plates—flat pieces of stone quarried in Bavaria and coated with asphaltum, one stone for each color. The negative had to be retouched by hand for each color, sometimes with fourteen different colors being used, then the stone exposed to sunlight for several hours before it was developed with turpentine. Each stone was hand-finished with the additional development of chosen areas using fine pumice powder before being etched in acid to reveal the image ready for printing. Special semitransparent inks were then used to transfer the image from the stones onto smooth paper, and finally each printed image was varnished to bring out its depth and richness.

The British Photochrom Company, with offices in London and Tunbridge Wells, published a series of twenty photochrome images of Rome, available to the public as prints for framing and as postcards. These and more than 5,000 other photochromes can be seen online at www.ushistoricalarchive.com/photochroms/index.html.

The Tempia di Vesta from the tourist souvenir *Ricordo di Roma Parte II* (opposite page, top); the Forum Boaria (opposite, bottom left) and Piazza Navona (opposite, bottom right) are 1900 photochromes.

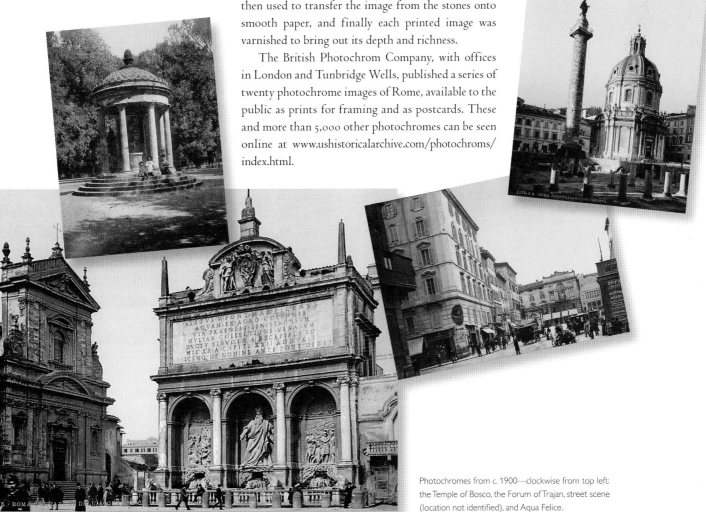

Photochromes from c. 1900—clockwise from top left: the Temple of Bosco, the Forum of Trajan, street scene (location not identified), and Aqua Felice.

THE TURBAYNE BINDINGS

When they launched the 20 Shilling Series of colored books in 1903, A&C Black knew full well that, in order to sell books at such a high price, the look of the book from the outside was just as important as the innovative color used on the inside.

American-born Albert Angus Turbayne moved to London in the early 1890s and established a close association with the pioneering bindery at the Carlton Studio. By 1903 his William Morris–inspired designs were considered to be the pinnacle of the bookbinder's art. His forte was the combination of exuberant blocking, often in three or four colors, and beautifully executed lettering, but one of the bindery's greatest skills was in creating designs that exactly matched the subject of the book. Albert Turbayne always did extensive research into his subject, consulting libraries and illustrated books to find precisely the right elements with which to illustrate each of the Black books.

The design details of the present series of Memories of Times Past books pay homage to the skills of the Turbayne Bindery. The designs in the side panels of the cover are derived from the original covers of the Black books, and the decorative elements within the book echo these designs, thus maintaining the theme and feel that Turbayne strove to achieve.

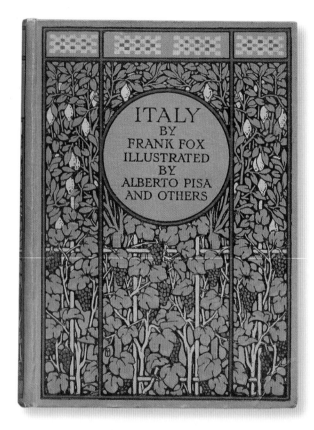

SOURCES, NOTES, AND CAPTIONS

The images used to complement the paintings come from a wide variety of sources, including books, postcards, museums, and libraries. They include photochromes, ephemera, advertisements, and maps of the period. The photochromes, and more than 5,000 others, can be seen online at www. ushistoricalarchive.com/photochroms/index.html. The large colored numbers refer to the plate numbers.

1 Left: Foro Romano—Avanzi del Tempio di Saturno, from *Ricordo di Roma, Parte II*. Right: Foro Romano—Tempio di Saturno, from *Roma, 32 Acquarelli*.

2 Top left: Panorama con Veduta del Colosseo, from *Ricordo di Roma Parte II*. Below: La Via dell'Impero, from a postcard c. 1932, reproduced in *Roma in Cartolina*.

3 Top: James Joyce in 1904, www.census.nationalarchives. com Below: Panorama del Foro Romano, from *Ricordo di Roma, Parte II*.

4 Top: Thomas Ashby, by Sir George Clausen. Bottom left: Arco di Settimo Severo, from *Ricordo di Roma, Parte II*. Top: collection of Roman coins—Publius Aelius Hadrianus, Sabina, and Roma.

5 Left: cover of *The Colour of Rome* by Olave Muriel Potter, illustrated by Yoshio Markino. Below right: 1902 postcard of Castel Sant'Angelo e Cupola di S. Pietro. Top right: Castel Sant'Angelo e Ponte Elio, from *Roma, 70 Vedute*.

6 Top left: holly, which was planted outside a house to offer protection to the inhabitants. Middle: eight columns of the Temple of Saturn, from *A History of Rome and the Roman People*, Vol. 1. Right: a 1900s postcard of the Forum.

7 Top left/below: cover and map from *Nuovissima Pianta di Roma*. Right: 1910 postcard of Roma—Arco di Costantino, Anfiteatro Flavio detto il Colosseo.

8 Left: Emperor Augustus, from *History of Rome* by Victor Duruy. Right: 1900s postcard, Roma—Tempio di Marte Ultor, from *Roma in Cartolina*.

9 Top left: statue of Vespasian. Below left: coin of Aureus Vespasianus. Right: Avanzi del Tempio di Saturno, from *Ricordo di Roma, Parte II*.

10 Main image: 1899 photochrome of the Colosseum. Above: silver tetradrachm of Vespasian, obverse and reverse.

11 Top right: "Colosseum by Torchlight, 1865," by Ippolito Caffi. Center: Anfiteatro Flavio o Colosseo, from *Roma, 70 Vedute*. Left: the Colosseum floodlit at night, iStockphoto.com.

12 Center: detail of stone carving on the Arch of Titus. Left: Foro Romano—Arco di Tito, from *Roma, 70 Vedute*. Right: Arch of Titus from Via Sacra, painting by Aubrey Waterfield, from *Rome and Its Story*.

13 Left: a 1905 postcard of Via Appia and Saint Sebastiano. Right: Sir Arthur Conan Doyle.

14 Left: a 1910 postcard of Il Palazzo dei Flavi. Right: View from the Palatine by Aubrey Waterfield, from *Rome and Its Story*.

15 Left: statue of Domitian, from Duruy's *History of Rome*. Center: remains of the library of the public palace, from Francis Wey's *Rome*. Right: a 1900s postcard of the Palatino Biblioteca.

16 Left: The Forum of Nerva by Aubrey Waterfield, from *Rome and Its Story*. Right: statue of Minerva, from Duruy's *History of Rome*, Vol. VII, Sect. II.

17 Left: Fontana di Trevi, from *Roma, 32 Acquarelli*. Center: film poster for *La Dolce Vita* by Frederico Fellini, starring Marcello Mastroianni and Anita Ekberg. Right: a 1905 one-cent coin and a 1915 ten-cent coin.

18 Left: Piazza Colonna by A. J. B. Thomas, from *Yesterday's Rome*. Below: Piazza Colonna, sepia wash drawing by Yoshio Markino, from *The Colour of Rome*. Right: Oscar Wilde.

19 Left: Il Pantheon, from *Roma, 32 Acquarelli*. Center: Il Pantheon, from *Roma, 70 Vedute*. Right: The Piazza of the Pantheon by Yoshio Markino, from *The Colour of Rome*.

20 Left: The Silversmith's Arch or Arcus Argentariorum, Porch of San Giorgio in Velabro, from Francis Wey's *Rome*. Top: Romulus and Remus republican coin. Right: coins of Settimo Severo.

21 Top: bronze medal of Horace, fourth century. Top left: modern photograph of the convent at Vicovaro, Flickr Creative Commons.

22 Left: Acquedotto di Claudia sulla via Appia Nuova, from *Roma, 70 Vedute*. Center: 1900s postcard of Campagna Romana Verso il Pascolo. Right: 1910 postcard of Claudio IV and the Aquedotto di Claudio.

23 Left: *Rome from the Villa Ludovisi*, an eighteenth-century painting by an unknown artist. Right: Campagna from Villa Pamphili Doria by Aubrey Waterfield, from *Rome and Its Story*.

24 Top: St. Benedict. Left: a modern photograph of Subiaco from the road to Sacro Speco, from almost exactly the same viewpoint as Alberto Pisa's painting, Flickr Creative Commons. Below: map of Rome and Subiaco, from *Baedeker's Central Italy*.

25 Top: the Subiaco coat of arms. Left: St. Scholastica.

26 Top: the holy stairs at the sacred grotto in Subiaco. Below right: fresco on the same staircase, showing death as a skeleton riding on a white horse with sword in hand. Below left: painting of St. Benedict on the curved ceiling of the lower church at Subiaco.

27 Left: 1900s postcard of women haymaking in the Roman countryside. Center: clouded yellow butterfly, from *Butterflies of the British Isles* by Richard South, Frederick Warne, 1906. Right: The Gleaner, from *Penrose's Pictorial Annual, 1913–14*.

28 Left: *St. Peter's from Villa Borghese*, by John Robert Cozens. Right: fountain in the Borghese Gardens, from Francis Wey's *Rome*.

29 Top left: map of Villa Borghese, from *Baedeker's Central Italy*, 1909. Below left: Tempio sui Lago di Villa Borghese, from *Roma, 70 Vedute*. Right: 1917 postcard of Roma—Villa Borghese—Il Laghetto.

30 Left: photograph of Anticoli Corrado, from *Picturesque Italy* by Kurt Hielscher, Brantano, 1925. Center: young woman of the Trastevere, from Francis Wey's *Rome*. Right: Oscar Kokoschka, detail from "The Dreaming Youths."

31 Left: 1573 engraving of the Villa d'Este, with people playing tennis on the courts to the right of the main building. Right: Garden of Villa d'Este, from *Rome, A Sketch Book* by Fred Richards.

32 Top: the coat of arms of Cardinal Scipione Borghese. Right: Villa Borghese—La Fontana, from *Roma, 70 Vedute*. Below: Villa Borghese from Roof Top by Aubrey Waterfield, from *Rome and Its Story*.

33 Left: 1899 photochrome of the Spanish Steps. Right: 1900s postcard showing the house where Keats lived at the bottom of the Spanish Steps on the Piazza di Spagna.

34 Center: Chiesa della Trinità dei Monti, from *Roma, 70 Vedute*. Left: 1906 postcard of the Spanish Steps and the Chiesa della Trinità dei Monti.

35 Left: a bronzed maiden, from Francis Wey's *Rome*. Top right: a photograph entitled "A View in Subiaco" from *Picturesque Italy* by Kurt Hielscher, Brantano, 1925. Below: Public Washhouse by Yoshio Markino, from *The Colour of Rome*.

36 Top: St. Catherine of Alexandria. Left: San Clemente by Aubrey Waterfield, from *Rome and Its Story*.

37 Top: 1908 postcard of "Costume della Campagna Romana." Right: Common Ragwort, from *Flowers of the Field* by Rev. C. A. Johns, Routledge, 1907. Below: Ploughing in Tuscany, in *From Sketchbook and Diary* by Elizabeth Butler, A&C Black, 1909.

38 Top: photograph of Subiaco, from *Picturesque Italy* by Kurt Hielscher, Brantano, 1925. Left: mural from Sacro Speco. Right: bell tower of Santa Scholastica (both photographs Flickr Creative Commons/Edith OSB).

39 Below left: Market of Piazza Navona, from Francis Wey's *Rome*. Top right: Male Greenfinch, from *Birds of Britain* by J. Lewis Bonhote, A&C Black, 1907. Below right: Campidoglio, from *Roma, 70 Vedute*.

40 Left: entrance to the Convent of the Ara Coeli, from Francis Wey's *Rome*. Right: Santa Maria in Ara Coeli by Yoshio Markino, from *The Colour of Rome*.

41 Left: "Benediction with Holy Child on Epiphany Day on the Steps of the Ara Coeli" by A. J. B. Thomas, from *Yesterday's Rome*. Right: interior of Santa Maria in Ara Coeli, from Francis Wey's *Rome*.

42 Top: The Lamb of God painted on the Dome of Stairs in Sacro Speco. Left: St. Benedict as a boy receives the habit, Sacro Speco (both photographs Flickr Creative Commons/Edith OSB).

43 A modern photograph of the chapel of San Lorenzo Loricato at St. Benedict, Subiaco; the viewpoint is the same as that for Pisa's painting.

44 Left: A Meeting on the Pincian—French and German Seminarists, from *From Sketchbook and Diary* by Elizabeth Butler. Right: Domenico and Sisto.

45 Left: a 1906 postcard of Piramide di Caio Cestio e Porta San Paolo. Right: Gate of San Paolo by Aubrey Waterfield, from *Rome and Its Story*.

46 Left: The Colosseum by Yoshio Markino, from *The Colour of Rome*. Below left: The Colosseum by Thomas Cole. Right: Colosseum detail, from a map in *Baedekers's Central Italy*.

47 Left: Arco di Tito, from *Ricordo di Roma, Parte II*. Right: Archi di Tito e Costantino—Ruine del Tempio di Venere e Roma, from *Roma, 32 Acquarelli*.

48 Left: a 1796 painting by Charles Louis Clerisseau of the Tivoli waterfalls. Right: A Street at Tivoli, from Francis Wey's *Rome*.

49 Left: a 1900s postcard of Tempietto Circolare in Villa Borghese. Right: Ilex Avenue in Villa Borghese by Aubrey Waterfield, from *Rome and Its Story*.

50 Main picture: Ponte Rotto by Gaspar Van Wittel, from *Yesterday's Rome*.

51 Top: St. Clemente, apse and central cross. Left: Pope Pius IX. Below right: Pulpit of the Epistle at St. Clemente, from Francis Wey's *Rome*.

52 Left: the *Bocca della Verità*, "the mouth of truth," at Santa Maria in Cosmedin. Top right: Santa Maria in Cosmedin, from Francis Wey's *Rome*. Below: Santa Maria in Cosmedin by Aubrey Waterfield, from *Rome and Its Story*.

53 Top: detail of the ceiling mosaic in San Prassede. Left: Chapel of San Zeno (both Flickr Creative Commons).

54 Left: "San Paolo after the Fire of 1823" by Francesco Diofebi, from *Yesterday's Rome*. Right: Basilica di San Paolo—Il Chlostro, from *Roma, 70 Vedute*.

55 Left: details of the floor mosaics in St. Maria di Cosmedin. Right: Benedictine Monk, by E. Duverger.

56 Left: the actress Adelaide Ristori, whose funeral mass was held in Santa Maria Sopra Minerva in 1906. Center: "St. Maria Sopra Minerva" (artist unknown), from *Yesterday's Rome*. Right: detail of a nineteenth-century painting of a religious ceremony in the presbytery of St. Maria Sopra Minerva, from *Yesterday's Rome*.

57 Top left: an 1899 photochrome of the Vatican. Below left: St. Peter's Dome and Fountain by Yoshio Markino, from *The Colour of Rome*. Below right: Piazza of St. Peter's by Aubrey Waterfield, from *Rome and Its Story*.

58 Left: "The Pope at Prayer Before the Statue of St. Peter" by A. J. B. Thomas. Right: "The Statue of St. Peter on St. Peter's Day," by A. J. B. Thomas; both from *Yesterday's Rome*.

59 Left: Cardinal Ippolito d'Este. Right: "In the Gardens of Villa d'Este" by Curzona Frances Louise Allport.

60 Left: map of Villa d'Este in Tivoli, from *Baedeker's Central Italy*, 1909. Center: Franz Liszt. Right: "Portrait of Liszt" by Istan Orosz, combining the head of Liszt with a view of the fountains at Villa d'Este.

61 Left: Remains of the Theater of Marcellus by Fred Richards, from *Rome, A Sketchbook*. Right: Teatro Marcello by Aubrey Waterfield, from *Rome and Its Story*.

62 Left: Isola Tiberia, from *Roma, 70 Vedute*. Right: The Tiber Island by Aubrey Waterfield, from *Rome and Its Story*.

63 Top left: *Ara Coeli Stairway from Capital Square* by A. J. B. Thomas, from *Yesterday's Rome*. Below left: Chiesa di San Maria Aracoeli, from *Roma, 70 Vedute*. Right: Santa Maria in Aracoeli by Fred Richards, from *Rome, A Sketchbook*.

64 Left: *The Steps of the Church of SS Domenico e Siste in Rome, 1906*, by John Singer Sargent. Right: Chapel of Saints Dominic and Sixtus, Wikipedia Commons.

65 Left: Santa Maria Maggiore, from *Roma, 32 Acquarelli*. Bottom right: Basilica di Santa Maria Maggiore, from *Roma, 70 Vedute*. Top right: 1899 photochrome of Santa Maria Maggiore.

66 Left: Foro Romano—Arco di Costantino, from *Roma, 70 Vedute*. Right: Arco di Costantino, from *Roma, 32 Acquarelli*.

67 Left: From the Loggia of San Angelo by Aubrey Waterfield, from *Rome and Its Story*. Right: The Castle of San Angelo by Yoshio Markino, from *The Colour of Rome*.

68 Main image: Campidoglio, from *Ricordo di Roma, Parte II*. Top right: 1899 photochrome of the Capitoline.

69 Left: Monte Pincio—Fontana dei Mosè, from *Roma, 70 Vedute*. Right: At the Gate of the Pincian by Yoshio Markino, from *The Colour of Rome*.

70 Top right: 1900s postcard of the Palatino and Circus Maximus. Below left: Santa Francesca and Forum by Aubrey Waterfield, from *Rome and Its Story*.

Tempio di Venere a Roma, from *Ricordo di Roma, Parte II*.

BIBLIOGRAPHY

Art in Rome from 1870 to 1900, Franco Borsi, Editalia, 1980.

Central Italy and Rome, Karl Baedeker, 1909.

The Colour of Rome, Olave Muriel Potter, Chatto and Windus, 1914.

The Conquest of Rome, Matilde Serao, New York University Press, 1992.

The Force of Destiny: A History of Italy Since 1796, Christopher Duggan, Allen Lane, 2007.

History of Rome and the Roman People, Victor Duruy, 1890.

Il Socialismo, May 1904.

Imagining Rome, Michael Liversidge and Catharine Edwards, Merrell Holberton, 1996.

Italy: An Illustrated History, Joseph Privitera, Hippocrene, 2000.

Italy and the Wider World, 1860–1960, Richard Bosworth, Routledge, 1996.

Peking to Paris: A Journey Across Two Continents in 1907, Luigi Barzini, Alcove, 1972.

Ricordo di Roma: 32 Acquarelli, A. Graldi, Milano, n.d.

Ricordo di Roma, Parte II, n.d.

Ricordo di Roma, 32 Vedute, Parte Prima, n.d.

Ricordo di Roma, 32 Vedute, Parte Seconda, n.d.

Ricordo di Roma, 70 Vedute, A. Scrocchi, Milano, n.d.

Roba di Roma, William Story, Houghton Mifflin, 1893.

Roma Beata, Maud How, Little, Brown, 1909.

Roma in Cartolina, Enrico Guidoni, Edizioni Kappa, 1984.

Roman Century, 1870–1970, J. P. Glorney Bolton, Hamish Hamilton, 1970.

Rome, Francis Wey, J. S. Virtue & Co., n.d.

Rome and Its Story, Lina Duff Gordon and St. Clair Baddeley, Dent, 1904.

Rome: A Sketchbook, Fred Richards, A&C Black, 1914.

The Story of Rome, Norwood Young, Dent, 1905.

Walks in Rome, Augustus Hare, Kegan Paul, Trench and Trübner, 1913.

Yesterday's Rome, Sergio and Glauco Cartocci, Plurigraf, 1977.

Piazza Navona painted by Aubrey Waterfield, from *Rome and its Story*.

THE TIMES PAST ARCHIVE

The Memories of Times Past series would be inconceivable without the massive Times Past Archive, a treasury of books, magazines, atlases, postcards, and printed ephemera from the golden age of color printing between 1895 and 1915.

From the time several years ago when the project was first conceived, the collecting of material from all over the world has proceeded in earnest. As well as a complete set of the ninety-two A&C Black 20 Shilling color books, which are the inspiration for the series, the archive houses full sets of period *Baedeker* and *Murray's Guides*; almost every color-illustrated travel book from illustrious publishing houses like Dent, Jack, Cassell, Blackie, and Chatto & Windus; and a massive collection of reference works with color plates on subjects from railways and military uniforms to wildflowers and birds' eggs.

The archive also contains complete runs of all the important periodicals of the time that contained color illustrations, including the pioneering *Penrose's Pictorial Annual: An Illustrated Review of the Graphic Arts*; the first-ever British color magazine, *Colour*; ladies' magazines like *Ladies' Field* and the *Crown*; and more popular titles such as *The Connoisseur* and the *London Magazine*.

These years were vintage years for atlas publishing, and the Times Past Archive contains such gems as Keith Johnston's *Royal Atlas of Modern Geography*, *The Harmsworth Atlas*, Bartholomew's *Survey Atlas of England and Wales*, and the *Illustrated and Descriptive Atlas of the British Empire*.

Last but not least, the archive includes a wealth of smaller items—souvenirs, postcards, tickets, programs, catalogs, posters, and all the colorful ephemera with which the readers of the original 20 Shilling books would have been familiar.

THE TIMES PAST WEB SITE

The Web site to accompany this project can be found at www.memoriesoftimespast.com, where you will find further information about the birth and development of the project, together with the complete original texts of titles published to date. There is also an area where you can take part in discussions raised by readers of the books who want to take their interest further and share their memories and passions with others. The Web site will start small and elegant, as you would expect of an "Edwardian Web site," but it will gradually become what you and we together make it, a place for devotees of art and culture from a century ago to meet and be inspired.

Palazzo Spada, painted by Aubrey Waterfield, from *Rome and Its Story*.

ILLUSTRATION CREDITS

Plate 43 main photograph, and Plate 26 photographs top and bottom right © Adrian Fletcher, www.paradoxplace.com.

UMBRIA

Castagnola — Ficulle — M.Martano — Ritaldi — Cappello — S.Cristine
M.Labro — S.Fiora — P.Centino — Brodo — M.Castello — Todi — Metelliana — Spoleto
Cana — Roccalbegna — Petricci — C.Viscardo — Morano — Colvalenza — Magliano — Renzano — Schei
M.Orgiali — Scansano — Acquapendente — Corbara — Civitella — Rosaro — Acquasparta — Ceselli
cia — Castel Giorgio — Orvieto — Bascha — Pesciano — Polenaco — Cesi — Ferentil
icole — Saturnia — Sovana — Sorano — S.Lorenzo — Porano — Castig — Guardea — Colcello — Collesecco — Strettura
Pereta — Pitigliano — Latera — Bolsena — lione — Alviano — S.Gemini — Collesci — Terni
gliano — Monciano — Valentano — L. di — Bagnorea — S.Michele — Lugnano — Morone
Marsiliana — Ischia — Bolsena — Celleno — Amelia — Papigni — Morro
Lagaccioli — Cap. — L. Bisentina — Celleno — Fastello — Grotte — S.Stefano — Attigliano — Penna — Narni — Stroncone — Greccio
Capalbio — di Monte — I.Martana — Montefiascone — Bomarzo — Itieli — Gualdo — Contigni
Orbetello — C.Ferriera — Cellere — Marta — Pianzano — Vitorchiano — Bassano — Orte — Otricoli — Calvi — Contigliano
Nunziatella — Casino — Tessenano — Bagnaia — Soriano — Bassanello — Gallese — Magliano — S.Benedetto
Port Ercole — Pescia — Montalto — Arlena — Toscanella — Viterbo — Bagnola — Aspra — S.Giovanni
Formica — L. di — S.Martino — Canepina — Vallerano — Vignanello — P.Felice — M.S.Giovanni
di-Burano — Chiarone — Burano — Castelluccio — Patrica — Borghetto — Cantalupo
Fiora — Vetralla — S.Giovanni — Caprarola — Ronciglione — Civita — Bonzano — P.Mirteto
Monte Romano — Capranica — Suri — Castellana — Filacciano — Montopoli
Corneto — Bieda — Barbarano — Nepi — S.Oreste — Fara — P.S.Loren
P.Clementino — Viano — Bassano-Suri — Monterosi — Rignano — P.Moj
Marta — Mignone — Oriolo — Trevignano — Baccano — Civitella — Correse — Nerola
Tolfa — Rota — Canala — Calcata — Campognano
S.Agostino — Allumiere — L. di — Castelnuovo — Leprignano — Moricone
Civitavecchia — Manziana — Bracciano — di Porto — Stazzano — M.Flavio
Stigliano — Bracciano — Anguillara — Palombara — Cantalupo
C.Linaro — S.Marinella — Sasso — Formello — M.Rotondo — Vicovar
Severa — S.M.a di — Isola Farnese — Mentana — Castel Mad
Furbara — Galera — La Storta — Marcigliana — Monterorbo — Ciciliano
Cerveteri — Tragliata — S.Onofrio — Tivoli — Ge
Palo — Palidoro — M.Mario — Capo Bianco — S.Gregorio — Poli
C.Guido — ROMA (ROME) — S.Lorenzo — Lunghezza — Castiglione — Gallicano
Magliana — Marcellini — Torrenuova — Zagarolo — Pa
Arrone — Maccarese — Sebastiano — Colonna — Cave
Fiumicino — P.Galera — T. di — C. di Morena — Frascati
Porto di Fiumicino — Porto — Mezzavio — Grotte Ferrata — Marino — Lugnano
Ostia — S.Giorgio — Rocca di Papa — Monte
Porcigliano — Solfaratella — Genzano — Palazzolo
Joining line with Pl.14 — Fontan di Papa — Albano — Nemi — Velletri
Tevere (Tiber) — Selva — M.Gio — Civita Lavinia — Cor
Ardea — Cisterna
S.Lorenzo — Campo Morto — C. di
Ferriera — Carroceto — Torre
Selva di Neno — Conca
Nettuno
P. di Anzio — Astura — Bocca